MW00484590

Praise for *Be the Brave One*

"Inviting, lively, accessible, provocative, and—dare I say—fun, Ann Kansfield's book is like sitting with your best friend, if your best friend is a faith-filled person who tells terrific stories and gives life-changing advice."

—James Martin, SJ, author of *Learning to Pray*

"Grab a beverage, find a comfortable spot, sit with this amazing, refreshing, candid, heart-opening, inspirational book. Ann Kansfield holds your hand, and guides you on a journey toward authentically living out your convictions, toward being the *brave one*, like her."

—The Rev. Jacqueline J. Lewis, PhD, senior
minister, Middle Collegiate Church

"The values, the ethics that Ann Kansfield brings in this book are the same ones she brings to her care for firefighters as an FDNY chaplain. As she shares stories of the city and of her role—stories of *being the brave one*—you'll discover insights so true, so down-to-earth, and so clear in their care for human lives, human spirits, that you'll be inspired to *be the brave one* too."

—Chief Vincent Dunn, former FDNY firefighter and author

"Ann Kansfield's unforgettable stories never disappoint, helping us learn courage, honesty, and faith from her without even realizing that we're learning. She is both completely unique and completely relatable. By the end of this book, she will feel like a wise and dear friend."

—Trisha Taylor and Jim Herrington, authors and
cohosts of *The Leader's Journey* podcast

"Ann Kansfield's story is the story of faith in action—of change and challenge as she follows Jesus on the streets and in the communities of her complicated home: New York, the 'City of God.'"

—Sara Miles, author of *Take This Bread: A Radical Conversion* and *City of God: Faith in the Streets*

"*Be the Brave One* is a rollicking romp through the wondrous calling of an urban pastor who navigates poop on the stoop, Hollywood stars in the sanctuary, and a couple thousand years of the heresy of homophobia in the church with equal parts hilarity and courage. Find yourself anchored by Ann Kansfield's faith and buoyed by her irreverence in this riveting read."

—Molly Baskette, senior minister of First Church Berkeley, UCC

"The insistent honesty of this book brings down barriers, helps us to listen, and in the end elicits something so sorely needed today: empathic imagination. I couldn't put this book down."

—Fred Harrell, founder and senior pastor of City Church San Francisco

BE THE BRAVE ONE

LIVING YOUR SPIRITUAL VALUES OUT LOUD
AND OTHER LIFE LESSONS

ANN KANSFIELD

WITH MARTY ST. GEORGE

Broadleaf Books
Minneapolis

BE THE BRAVE ONE
Living Your Spiritual Values Out Loud and Other Life Lessons

Copyright © 2021 Ann Kansfield. Printed by Broadleaf Books, an imprint of 1517 Media. All rights reserved. Except for brief quotations in critical articles or reviews, no part of this book may be reproduced in any manner without prior written permission from the publisher. Email copyright@1517.media or write to Permissions, Broadleaf Books, PO Box 1209, Minneapolis, MN 55440-1209.

Scripture throughout is taken from the New Revised Standard Version Bible, copyright © 1989 National Council of the Churches of Christ in the United States of America with several adaptions for contemporary wording by the author/coauthor. Used by permission. All rights reserved worldwide.

This is a work of nonfiction, with events and conversations recounted and reconstructed from memory and may not reflect exact wording. This work represents the author(s) perspective, where events and details might be remembered and recounted differently by others.

In instances where seeking permissions or personal releases were warranted, the author(s) claim due diligence. In the rare instance where responses were not received, for such parties requesting changes in the text, these will be incorporated into subsequent editions.

Cover image: Shutterstock
Cover design: Laura Drew

Print ISBN: 978-1-5064-6373-5
eBook ISBN: 978-1-5064-6374-2

CONTENTS

CONTENTS

FOREWORD

As I sat down on the last day of Pride week to compose a foreword for Reverend Ann's book, I noticed that the song playing was a lively upbeat version of the Burt Bacharach/Hal David song: "What the World Needs Now is Love." How appropriate, I thought, for a host of reasons, especially in this time of divisiveness, fear and so much anger.

I met Pastor Ann when I returned to the New York City Fire Department (FDNY) as Fire Commissioner in 2014. I had retired in 2002 as the Chief of the Department after almost 33 years in uniform and was elated to be back. We had a Chaplain vacancy and Ann came to my office to interview for the position. I am still not sure who interviewed who? We had a long conversation and I felt that I had re-connected with an old friend, although we had never previously met. Ann's positivity and enthusiasm are contagious. Early in our talk I knew that I need not interview any other candidates. She was the one—our first female and our first gay Chaplain.

The members of our Department are known as The Bravest (Firefighters) and The Best (EMS), and that they are. They are hard-working, dedicated and selfless.

They have taken their time though to be as accepting of differences as they now are. If I go back in time, almost 52 years ago to 1969, when I began my career in the FDNY, pre-EMS, we were an entirely male and overwhelmingly white workforce. There was a provision in our rules and regulations citing "moral turpitude," a somewhat vague group of offenses that, at that time, included homosexuality. Moral turpitude could lead to discipline and even loss of your job. There were no openly gay members for much of my early career and still today there are few (or at least few who are open about it).

So, why did I think this would be a good idea to bring this openly gay, female Protestant pastor into our predominantly male, Roman Catholic, straight organization and think it would all work out? After just an hour together I was 100% certain that she would be a perfect fit. And she was and continues to be. Her gift, her magic is her openness that invites us to be open. Her personal bravery fits perfectly with our Department which prides itself on bravery. Notwithstanding all the work she does outside of her Chaplaincy with us, she is tireless in her efforts to serve our 17,000 members as if each of them is the most valuable individual in her congregation.

Her book paints a picture of one of New York City's greatest assets: A true pastor to those in need, nourishing us literally and figuratively. And as for her service to our Department, she has been with us at our happiest times and our darkest hours, and she has become one of us in the truest sense. She is one of The Bravest and The Best.

Daniel A. Nigro,
Fire Commissioner,
New York City Fire Department

INTRODUCTION

I didn't set out toward transformation—it happened slowly. From a run-of-the mill capitalist jerk who spent her young life masquerading as someone she clearly wasn't, I became a reasonably content married lesbian pastor with a couple of kids and a three-ring circus of a church in a relatively obscure part of Brooklyn. I don't think I was even aware of the change. But, over time, I've grown into this new life, a life I embrace as a gift from God. It's not a life without its tragedies, pandemics, and young children vomiting in the wee hours, but all of it is part of the gift.

I'm a small-town pastor in a big city. I don't mean that I come from a small town, I mean there's a small-town sensibility to my life in the city. A sense of community and ordinary moments of grace. I'm surrounded by God's people, some I've known for decades, and others I've only just met. We may have vastly different values, but we share a belief that values matter, that they are what build and hold a life together. Discovering and naming those essential guides has been part of what's led to this transformation.

I didn't think much about my own personal values until I attended a retreat a few years ago where the leader challenged us to come up with a list. I took the assignment to heart. When I got home, I wrote out my list of values on a whiteboard and then took a picture of it with my phone. Later, at lunch with a friend, I'm not sure what compelled me to share, but in the time between the waiter taking our sandwich orders and returning with the food, I found myself somewhat awkwardly reading aloud phrases like *When you're in a hole, stop digging* and *Be the brave one*. I felt vulnerable, like I was oversharing— a tip-off that those mainstays were deeply personal and said a lot about me and what matters most to me.

My friend seemed intrigued. She wanted to know how I defined those values, where I saw them at play in my life, and what kind of a difference they made. At first, I thought they were just quick ideas, personal notes. But truly naming those things that are essential, good, and true, and intentionally leaning into them, made a huge difference in my life.

■ ■ ■

Several years have gone by and those same values have become my go-to principles to live by. Putting them into practice has been an adventure, a way to live their timeless truths in my everyday life. They have held fast through fires, lost loved ones, fierce winds, and a chaplaincy for first responders during one of the largest early waves of the pandemic in the city.

Take, for example, attempting to live *authentically*. We all wear masks in life—I don't mean masks for a pandemic, but masks to hide ourselves in order to protect us from judgment or rejection. As a kid, I hid a lot. I tried so hard to fit in with the others, but I was decidedly not cool. No amount of trendy makeup or fashionable dresses could hide the fact that femininity eluded me. Hiding myself meant playing a small game, and it wasn't a fun game. As a result, I wasn't a party to be around. My lack of authenticity kept people at arm's length. It's only when I began to embrace who I really was—the honest, fraught, vulnerable, and deeply human person—that I began truly experiencing life. As I practiced sharing my authentic self with others, I noticed people sharing more of themselves with me. If I shared my real self, others would share their real selves with me. And in this process, life around me became . . . well . . . more alive.

Before you think, *values*, really? I know, it's a word everyone uses (some even for political purposes), and yet it's clear not everyone has the same definition. Conservative Christians might lose their shit if they discovered I live by values. So, what are they? Traditions? Principles? Maybe both. For me, they're what comes from living from a place of deep conviction. Some might call them "faith" values. For me, they are simply anchors: they hold me to what's true.

I kind of think of values as a code you live by—a basic framework of principles that anchor you to what's true and important. You've heard of the Guy Code, right? (If not, look it up on *Urban Dictionary*.) The Guy Code consists of rules like, *Don't date your friends' sisters* or *When your buddy's girlfriend asks where he is, the only acceptable answer is "I have no idea."* Or, the Girl Code: *Don't date your friend's ex without asking permission.* You get the idea. Pretty dumb rules, but they represent basic guiding principles. Don't think of this book as a Girl Code or even an Ann Code, but as a way to understand your own true ground, your God Code, with these anchors as a possible starting point. Each chapter highlights a different code, a way to live that can help bring us closer to God. Whatever you call your own set of values, I hope this book helps you start to consider making a list, maybe even drawing it up on your own whiteboard.

The basis for these values came from a simple question: *How can I live my life the way that Jesus would, if Jesus were living my life?* (This is a phrase my friends Trisha Taylor and Jim Harrington have used.) If you grew up evangelical in the early 1990s, you might have worn a WWJD bracelet on your wrist. When faced with a difficult choice, good Christian kids everywhere would look to the bracelet and think, *What would Jesus do?* Modeling values after Jesus seemed like a great plan. But in the spring of 1994, I looked anxiously toward my WWJD bracelet for guidance about which college to attend and for how to think about my sexual orientation, and immediately discovered its limitations. Jesus never went to high school in America, and he totally failed to take the SAT. And when it comes to sexual orientation, Jesus didn't really offer much guidance. In fact, according to the biblical text, Jesus didn't say anything about it.

It's hard to envision living the same life as a man who lived two millennia ago, but I took my imagination for a ride and tried to picture Jesus living my life, here and now, and I started to see something different. I began to think he'd greet people on my Brooklyn street with a welcoming smile and offer up a silent prayer for the people surrounding him in the subway. He'd also use hair products and deodorant, if at all possible. At least, he would if he were living my life, because he might be schlepping boxes of veggies for the food pantry, fixing broken stuff in the church, or meeting celebrities over piles of human poop on the church steps.

This is a book about values and Jesus and transformation—and also about other related things, like holy shit. Here's the miracle: an ordinary person heading to work on Wall Street one day can begin offering silent prayers on the subway and realize that everything is holy. She can have a vision of Jesus-in-my-shoes that transforms her from a competitive striver moving up the ladder of financial success to a city neighborhood pastor feeding the hungry.

This is a book about living out of your convictions and how that radically changes us and those around us. It starts with identifying your values. And listen, if it's important for you to not use the word *values* (and you'd rather the right-wing fundagelicals keep it for themselves), use a different term—principles, anchors, God Code—and there you have it, "values" without judgment or shame.

Any pastor knows that you cannot let the minute details of a story get in the way of a good lesson (which is also why pastors are known for using the "fish story" strategy when offering their real-life parables). So, it's important to add here that many names and events have been factually altered to streamline the lessons, to combine stories, and to honor the privacy of individuals—as well as to leave a little room for the fish story. (And both in the stories and in the fish-additions, I have sought to keep integrity about sharing stories that are not mine, leaving out those that are also not mine to tell. I hope in respect to others' stories that I got it right.)

Finally, a warning. If you're having trouble following the flow and multiple options and themes and word choices, reading this book may be a bit of a meandering ride. (Meandering *is* actually part of the Ann Code.) I tend to wander off a bit. It's how my brain is wired. At times, it feels like fireworks exploding, firing hundreds of little bits of colorful lights into the sky. I get sidetracked easily, but I've discovered that's often when the adventure is the most exciting, and when having anchors can be very helpful.

Over time, I've practiced living out these principles so often, and in so many settings, they feel as natural to me as breathing. It's like learning any new skill: In the beginning it's hard and requires conscious attention. Sometimes it feels awkward and difficult, and often I forget or make mistakes. With time, attention, and practice, though, it becomes part of my life. And then, just when I think I've really got it, I see new ways I haven't been fully living out those values and the process continues.

Finally, a thank you. One of the anchors that's been a lifeline for me is the idea that everything is fixable. And because of my mind/body wandering and trying to stay on track, I fixed *this* problem of writing a book by working with a kick-ass coauthor, Marty. I wrote the book via Facebook-like posts and texts and Marty became the organizing principle. Our fix created a new, exciting way to co-write a book. Which leads me to the first chapter: *Work with What You've Got.*

1

WORK WITH WHAT YOU'VE GOT

Authenticity

As a kid, I didn't fit in well at school. I was awkward. I was gender messy, even as early as the third grade. So, as you might expect, I was bullied mercilessly. I tried to be authentic, but think back with me to the third grade. Being *authentic* was always the wrong answer. My classmates wanted conformity, and I knew what I needed to do. If I conformed to the cool girls, I could get by—yet, even at the age when peer pressure reigned supreme, I couldn't do it. I was different in so many wild and wonderful ways. For one, I liked church. And I didn't have as much money as my classmates, so I didn't have cool clothes. There was a poster in the nurse's office that showed a bunch of roosters and one of them had a real hair comb. It read: *Dare to be Different*. I looked at that poster every time I went to the nurse, and thought, *Eff that; I don't like being different.* I wasn't willing to pay the price to be cool, so I conformed. But I never fit in. Neither the girls nor guys in my class knew what to make of me.

■ ■ ■

I came by my small-town sensibility honestly. I was born in Holland, Michigan, a little Dutch Sim-City founded in the mid-1800s by Calvinist immigrants from the Netherlands. They rebuilt their new home in true Dutch tradition, bringing their church and their traditions with them. A Dutch Reformed Church sits in the middle of town, a Dutch windmill near a tributary, and many streets are lined with tulips. I have childhood memories of the town, and also of leaving it. When the big truck pulled up to our house, "United Van Lines" written across the side, I naturally assumed it was a Dutch name and couldn't understand why the driver didn't answer when I called him Mr. Van Lines. You can imagine how Rochester was going to be a culture shock to a seven-year-old.

By age ten, I was pretty sure I was going to be a baseball player, but at the same time, I *really* loved church. As a pastor's daughter, I tagged along when my dad preached at various congregations. There is a tradition in our denomination called "pulpit supply," which means you were available to take a spot on a pulpit when needed. (This also allowed pastors to occasionally take a vacation!) Churches loved my father, not just for what he preached but because he was a fresh voice. I loved going with him. I was an extroverted kid and I felt special traveling on pulpit supply trips. Plus, the arrival of a child with the guest preacher was a novelty, and I loved the attention. We visited a wide variety of churches and, since the seminary where my dad worked was ecumenical, I was continually exposed to different faith traditions. I also had a rating system for the quantity and quality of the after-church cookies and drinks, and soon had my own list of favorite spots.

Not fitting in at school. Geeking out on a love for church. Seeing a school poster laughably tell me to be different. All of this contributed to a young life humming in stress. The fact that my most consistent place of comfort was our little church in Rochester, the First Reformed Church, is a bit of a miracle. It wasn't a hippy-dippy, liberal kind of place. It was pretty typical. We did the usual churchy things. At this point in my life, I wasn't sure if I was queer or not, but I was sure of *one* thing: I did *not want to be queer*. I could be a tomboy, I could be awkward, I could be quirky, I could be gender-messy, but I could *not* be gay.

My desperation to not be gay didn't originate in church, but came from a totally unexpected place. When I was little, I would wake up early on Sunday mornings.

My parents, in the continual quest of all parents, just wanted to sleep, so they let me watch TV—but only religious programs like *Davey and Goliath* and *Bible Quiz*. But then I happened to watch *The 700 Club*, which was unusually effective at teaching me, and anyone else watching, that if we were queer it would not end well for us, or for the church, or for all of America.

Even in my awkwardness and non-conformity, the Rochester congregation loved me just the way I was. They probably didn't spend a lot of time thinking about the real me, but they saw someone different, and they helped me on the path to being myself, being authentic. Their love helped me survive the terrible teens. And while I was afraid they might catch on to my being gay (and thus bring the downfall of America), I also realized that they were the ones who helped me learn about God and Jesus and hospitality and love.

What I learned at that church gave me a God Code, an anchor. I knew that whatever my life looked like, moving forward, I was loved, authentically: cookie list, tomboy, baseball player. I learned authenticity despite working so hard to avoid that rooster poster. It was that value that led to a later move to New York City, to my abandoning a lucrative Wall Street career, and to entering seminary after 9/11. Authenticity was the anchor that held me as I learned who I was and how to begin walking that out.

2

AUTHENTICITY IS A PATH. SAYING YES IS A START TO THAT PATH.

Authenticity

If you ask any New Yorker about their experience living through September 11, they will invariably mention the weather. In New York City, 9/11 was the most beautiful day—sunny, warm, perfectly clear blue skies. On that infamous day, my personal quest had led me right into the heart of New York City.

Though I loved the church and was a pastor's daughter, I was also a competitive striver. Call it a way to mask the insecurities of not fitting in, or sheer determination, or still learning to hold to that anchor of authenticity, or heck, just call it the single best path to making a lot of money. Throughout my adolescence, I honed my competitive striver skills; I got into an Ivy League college with the assumption that I was going to be either a doctor or a lawyer. I had no interest in science or biology, but I did like to argue, so I knew my path: law school.

However, after having real challenges with the SAT, I was terrified of taking the LSAT.

As college graduation approached, my mom called to remind me that my student loans would be due in a few short months.

"What are your plans, Annie?"

"Ummm . . ."

I knew I needed a job. I was going to college in New York City, and at least a quarter of my graduating class went to work on Wall Street. A friend suggested I give it a try and coached me through my first interview. He loaned me a fancy watch and an elegant fountain pen so that I could look like a stockbroker, even though I had no idea what a stockbroker actually did. I went and interviewed, armed with the pen and watch, and I got the job. It felt good to tell people I worked on Wall Street. I promptly upgraded my wardrobe, adding several power suits and buying myself a Coach attaché case so everyone would know that I was making it. Because apparently nothing says "I'm important" like a blazer and a leather bag. It was the antithesis of authenticity, but it was part of the path.

Over the next several years, I would take the subway from my apartment in Park Slope to the financial district. Though I hadn't ever considered working in the financial services industry until the day I interviewed for the job, I took to the Wall Street lifestyle. The work involved intense focus for short amounts of time (which suited my natural attention span challenges), and there were plenty of opportunities for competition. The dot-com boom had created a euphoric atmosphere. I worked for an online brokerage firm in the midst of rapid expansion with lots of opportunities for career advancement. Best of all, I felt important. (Again, not a lesson in kick-ass values, but there it is.)

As the firm outgrew its Wall Street headquarters, my team moved into a "swing space" on the 23rd floor of Two World Trade Center. The building seemed magical, especially the shopping mall that occupied the space under the two towers. One of the new mall stores still under construction was a Victoria's Secret. The front windows had been covered over, presumably to ensure that we didn't actually *learn* Victoria's secret until they were ready to reveal it to us, but also to offer the construction workers privacy. In place of the usual butcher paper, this soon-to-be opening Victoria's Secret covered their windows with mirrors. So, instead of seeing contractors at work making the space ready for bras and panties, we saw ourselves reflected in the windows.

I hadn't noticed this new setup as I rushed by on my way to work. But one morning as I passed, I saw someone who appeared to be quite a handsome guy. In fact, I even said to myself, *Wow! What a good-looking dude.* And just as I finished the thought, I realized, *Oh shit, that's me! Even I think I look like a guy.* In that moment my inclination was to beat myself up. I certainly didn't have a balanced self-image. But, at the same time, I could not deny that I thought the person I saw reflected in the mirror was good looking. It reminded me that just seeing ourselves, our real selves, as God sees us was important. Not anticipating what we might look like but surprising ourselves with what we actually see.

Another lesson in authenticity: God sees us through lenses we can't always imagine. I had created a self-image that was consistent with that of a striver, a Wall Street "Master of the Universe" and a cutthroat finance person. But the ability to see myself through another lens, through Victoria's unintended lens, was the beginning of the process of seeing myself in new ways, through multiple lenses, viewed at multiples angles. And ultimately, it led me to align those views with the reality of how God saw me. And maybe, just maybe, that is Victoria's *real* secret.

Don't get me wrong; at that time, my personal lens still said I was an investment banker, but that mirror told me something more. I liked Wall Street, but there was part of my identity that needed to be looked at more fully. And yet another part of me that still loved church. (That handsome person in the mirror would look fine in a collar.) I thought maybe I should take a step toward the person in the mirror.

New Brunswick Theological Seminary has a campus in Queens. I took a class called "Introduction to the Bible" and attacked it like a striver who was also a preacher's kid. However, I quickly learned that the deck was stacked against me. First, long intricate Bible passages are inconsistent with my ADHD. Second, my fellow classmates were intimidating. I was surrounded by church ladies who had seemingly studied the Bible from infancy. I worked my hardest to dig into the text, but I was no match for the church ladies. They excelled on the tests. I was lucky to scrape out a C, a grade that was just not consistent with my striver mentality, and for that reason, my time at New Brunswick was going to be one-and-done.

Frankly, as much as I felt the calling to seminary, I was still worried about prestige and cash and external affirmation. Working on Wall Street met all those needs. Well, I thought it did. Wisdom from the rearview mirror tells me that authenticity is one part knowing what your calling is, and one part knowing what it isn't. But at that point, I was still an Ivy Leaguer-slash-banker, and I was also appropriately ambitious. I had already left my first firm for a job at an investment bank, working for a branch manager whose office managed a good bit of money for his own investment clients. The deeper I got into his operation, the more I started to realize he wasn't the most ethical operator in the business, and I realized that I needed to move on.

On Monday, September 10, 2001, I quit that job. And with all the confidence of a young striver, I had already started the process of finding a new one. Wall Street was still hot, and I had no trouble finding openings. On September 11, the next day, I had an interview scheduled at a different office of the same investment firm, at 99 Wall Street. I called that morning, bright and early, to confirm the interview time. The woman at the office informed me that a few blocks away two planes had hit the World Trade Center. The interview was postponed.

The New Yorkers of September 11, both natives and adoptive, were profoundly impacted by the attacks. Each of us can tell you exactly where we were and what we did that day. By the end of the day, we were all inextricably bonded as a community in the terror of the attacks. Later, in talking to many of my friends, I realized that in the immediate aftermath of the attacks, we all responded in our unique ways. Some of us were glued to the TV, not sure of what would happen next. Some of us rushed out of Manhattan. Some rushed to help. One friend decided to go home and clean his apartment, not an activity that normally rose to the top of his priority list. Me? I felt a drive to do my civic duty. Or just something that seemed "normal" when everything had changed. New York was holding a primary election, and no terrorist was going to keep me from voting—I went to vote in an election that was ultimately canceled.

Over time, 9/11 impacted everyone differently. People's worlds, their values, changed. Some immediately, others started shifting perspectives and, item by item, made life changes. In my case, not only was there no job interview, there was no longer a job for me at that investment firm, or any investment firm. 99 Wall Street, a good three-quarters of a mile from Ground Zero, was covered with dirt and dust, and in the middle of the exclusion zone. Nobody was allowed in or out of that area for several months, as New Yorkers started the process of cleaning Lower Manhattan. Years later, another crisis, the pandemic, would reshape and shut down the city with a similar magnitude, impacting people's worlds and how they lived their values. But this was 9/11, 2001.

As an unemployed striver at that time, I felt useless. All the money in the world was useless. All the prestige I thought I had built was gone. It would have been useless anyway. My fancy Coach bag? Useless. Yes, I was a regular churchgoer, but it became clear that my god was also prestige. I worshipped affirmation: from the church, from the world, and from New York City. And to me, New York City affirmation meant financial success. That fall of 2001 became my own "Saul on the road to Damascus" experience: when it felt like the whole world was falling apart, I no longer wanted to conquer the inconsequential world of financial services. I didn't care about the money, or the Coach bag, or the fancy pen. I just wanted to be in church. Real church. Not just the church of my affirmation.

Unlike Saul's experience—flashing light, falling, blindness, Jesus—my epiphany didn't come out of nowhere. While I worked on Wall Street, I was attending church and leading a youth group every Thursday. On Thursday, September 13, I wanted to be with them, but the subways weren't running yet. My need to be at church, with church, about church became an obsession. On September 18, I cold-called my professor from Bible class and asked him whether I could talk with him about enrolling in seminary again. Assuming I had missed the fall cutoff, I expected him to tell me spring semester started in January. However, he said, "Yes, the semester has already started, but given what happened we had to cancel the first week of classes. We start fresh this week. Let me pick you up at four and I'll drive you to your first class."

And just like that, I was a seminarian.

I had finally recognized something true in me and about me. And with this change I started on the path of intentional authenticity. It's an age-old story; I had a path in mind, but God had a different path. Once I was able to lift the blinders from my eyes, I also realized that living authentically required a course correction. In this case, a pretty large one.

That direction change didn't just change my career; it impacted every single part of my life. Much later it was that same value that led me to Jen, who is now my wife. I had known her by sight, from—where else—church. While I was attending seminary at New Brunswick Theological, I worked part-time as interim pastor at Flatlands Reformed Church in Brooklyn. I also continued to attend my home church, Middle Collegiate Church in Manhattan. Not only did Jen attend Middle Collegiate, she and I both used to work at World Trade Center. In fact, we would see each other on our commutes and say to ourselves, "One of these days I should say hello to that woman from Middle Collegiate," but we never did.

Such is life in New York. You can see the same people on your commute every day but not know their names or what they do. And invariably, at some point they would just disappear, like a miniature urban rapture. After a few months, something would remind you of that person and you would say, "Geez, I haven't seen them in months. I wonder what happened to them?" And you would never know. It was one of the mysteries of living in a city of nine million people. I refer to it as "The First Time I Didn't Meet Jen."

Jen grew up Southern Baptist and she also loved church. However, as she would later share with me, Jen knew that as a woman in that denomination, her highest aspiration within church would have been to be a pastor's wife. She also knew that being married to a man wasn't for her, and unfortunately, that was a mix that led her to become an alcoholic at a young age. She did an ignominious tour of various state colleges in California and ended up with a low GPA—college was not made for alcoholics. Eventually she graduated, got sober, and realized she had a calling for ministry. She applied to Union Theological Seminary, but given that her transcript was a bit of a mess, she was rejected.

Meanwhile, she had started teaching a Sunday school for three-year-olds at Middle Collegiate, and in the middle of the school year, when she received the rejection from Union, she was thrown into a depression so deep she was unable to get herself to church.

At the panic-stricken request of the associate minister, I agreed to continue teaching that class until Jen felt up to coming to church again. Which for me was almost impossible. Three-year-olds can't be reasoned with.

They don't make sense. I was supposed to be teaching them something about God and Jesus (or really just keeping them alive for an hour) and all they kept saying was, "Where's Jen?" and "We want *Jenn*ifer!" Unlike me, I figured this Jennifer person must be wonderful with three-year-olds. My teaching stint lasted just a few weeks, but those Sundays were an abject disaster. I vowed that once this mysterious Jen person came back, I would never, ever teach toddlers again. Many times I've wished I had Jen's supposed gifts with young children, but eventually I realized that I have my own talents, and I can't beat myself up for that particular shortcoming—also a lesson in authenticity.

Fast forward a year. I was progressing in my studies at New Brunswick and continued working part-time as a youth pastor at Middle Collegiate. The associate pastor mentioned that a friend of hers named Jennifer, the same Jen who had made me teach three-year-olds, wanted to talk with me as she was interested in attending seminary but was concerned about being gay. We arranged to meet at Bryant Park where we walked and talked for over two hours. Then we did it again a few days later. I suggested she visit me at the seminary, and I would introduce her to my dad who was the president of the seminary and could answer her questions.

The morning she came to the seminary I was excited to show her around, wanting to make sure she got a good impression of the place. She booked an appointment with my dad, but he had completely forgotten about it and was out of town that day. I was mortified. And totally delighted. I showed her around the seminary myself and we chatted all afternoon. She decided to apply to New Brunswick. I was disappointed to think that might be the end of our meetings, but the following week Jen sent me an email inviting me to go with her to the Brooklyn Botanical Garden. I immediately forwarded the email to my butch buddy for a deep analytical reading to see if it was a date or not. After a lengthy etymological analysis, it was determined that it was most definitely a date. We went to see the cherry blossoms and started dating after that.

One Sunday after church I was driving up Flatbush Avenue, eating a snack with one hand while changing out of my clergy shirt and into a different shirt with the other, to go on a date with a woman I realized I was starting to fall in love with. That moment, I knew I had leveled up as a New Yorker. Things were changing at life-altering speed: 9/11, seminary, interim work with a church, Jen. And me. I was looking at myself for the first time and seeing not only Victoria's secret but my own. I was growing into a truer understanding of my authentic self, and of what being anchored by values meant.

3

GO BIG OR GO HOME

Courage

In that fall of 2001, when I concluded I'd never go back to financial services, as much as I loved being in seminary, I knew it didn't pay the bills. Seminary *sent* me bills. I needed a job.

In October, my friend Souci called me and said, "You're going to hear from a guy named Carl from the Health Insurance Plan of New York. He's going to interview you, he's going to offer you a job, and you're going to take it."

That job didn't sound like me at all.

"Souci, I appreciate it. I'm done with financial services, but I don't think that job is for me. I'm going to seminary."

She said, "That's fine, but while you study, you are going to take this job."

She was right. The job was a gift—twenty hours a week working with volunteers who taught a program for people with chronic health conditions. It wasn't what I had ever imagined doing, but I learned how to recruit and train volunteers. I attended classes in the evening and studied on the Jersey Transit train. Not only did it help me pay for seminary, it funded my passion for preaching.

■ ■ ■

As an out, gay woman, I had never really expected to serve a church. I had been excited to enter the seminary, but I didn't see a clear path laid out for my future. As I began to understand the value of authenticity, I moved in the direction of my calling and gifts. But in that area of my life, "Go Big or Go Home" was a completely foreign value to me. I knew what it meant on Wall Street: nice pens, expensive briefcases, entertaining clients, and conspicuous consumption. Now that I was moving into a completely different vocation, the idea wasn't as well developed.

Part of the reason why I hadn't wanted to go to seminary was my legitimate fear that an actual church—a congregation of people—would not want to hire an out gay pastor. Or even worse, that a decision to call a gay pastor might divide a congregation. As a result, when I finally committed to seminary, I made a deal with God: I would attend, but I wasn't going to actually be a pastor of a congregation. After all, it felt like a complete impossibility for someone who was out and gay. Plus, it was just far too fraught. The only vision I had for what it could look like was when Rev. Janie Spahr, a gay pastor, was called to the Downtown Presbyterian Church in Rochester. I was a freshman in high school at the time; it was a very formative memory, mostly because it was huge news, making the front page in the Rochester papers, and there was a ton of controversy about it. I knew there were people who were very upset by her being called. Even though I didn't realize I was gay at the time, I was sure that it would be impossible to be gay and a pastor of a congregation, or that, at the very least, it would involve church drama and possible rejection.

So, it came as a surprise when the Reformed Church of Flatlands reached out to me after my first year in seminary. Flatlands was a congregation of about seventeen, many of them from the Caribbean Islands. A historic church, it was the first of its kind in Brooklyn. Their longtime pastor was about to retire, and they were scrambling to find someone to fill in quickly. Like the "pulpit supply" of my father's profession, I moved into somewhat familiar territory. In fact, although this was the beginnings of my path toward going big, I'm not sure I would have pursued it without my warm feelings about pulpit supply. Being a pastor? Scary. Stepping in for an absent pastor, meeting the church matriarchs, and eating the cookies after church? That felt eminently comfortable. I couldn't help but get excited. I worked hard on my sermons and got them done early, completely written out, and practiced over and over. I fell in love with the people, and I also fell in love with being a neighborhood pastor.

Because I was a pastor still in seminary, I was assigned a mentor. Rev. Dan Ramm was the pastor of the Flatbush Reformed Church, a mile or two up Flatbush Ave from the Flatlands church. Dan would call me every Monday to review how things went on Sunday, and how things were going in general. After the first month or two, the consistory (yes, that's the rather particular term for the board of the congregation in the Reformed Church) decided to keep me on for the year. They would bring in someone ordained to officiate at communion, but everything else, I would do. When I got my first paycheck, I couldn't believe someone was actually paying me to do something that came so easily to me it could hardly be considered *work*.

As I said yes to these new opportunities, I also began to see that the principles guiding me—authenticity, going big, courage, and so on—weren't just *in* me but operating all around me. Maybe that's why I also think of them as God Code. They derive from somewhere deeper, beyond me, and as I recognize specific values that are particular to me, I name them and understand them as the values I live by. Those values made the difference in how I viewed myself, who I saw in the mirror, and what a paycheck meant, no matter the size. Wall Street never gave me so much. And the best part was that these values came to me in a way that made it natural and organic for me to accept them. If I had looked at my entire path, from Holland to Brooklyn, I could see dozens of places where I could have easily abandoned the journey if I'd known how long it would take and how difficult the challenges would be. However, through the grace of God, the path that had been unclear to me became visible—one hill at a time. And the more hills I climbed, the more confidence I gained to conquer the next one.

Over the course of the year, the congregation at Flatlands grew. I joked that it was like fishing in a barrel because there just weren't a lot of churches in the area. Although Brooklyn is covered with subway lines, Flatlands is the closest thing Brooklyn has to being "off the grid," and that isolation was a gift. Eventually, though, the church consistory decided to call an ordained minister, and I hadn't been ordained yet. When the news came, I was devastated and unsure if any other church would have me. Throughout my time at Flatlands, I remained closeted. It didn't feel good, but I felt I needed to keep my mouth shut. I'm sure people suspected, but it became a don't ask, don't tell situation. Not speaking out weighed on my soul. I wasn't convinced the church wanted to know, and I also felt I wasn't being fully truthful.

By my last Sunday, we had over fifty people attending services, and at my going away party, we had at least seven different Caribbean chicken dishes (aka "the holy bird"). I was crestfallen about someone else being called to Flatlands—I really loved them. When the new pastor offered for me to stay on as an associate pastor, I was too emotionally drained to think it through properly. I delegated it to a group of my fellow seminarians, and they thought it was a terrible idea. They discerned that this striver would make a terrible Number Two after having been the solo pastor.

Authenticity and courage are values that I've grown to embrace and values I've grown into. Every step has revealed the cost of speaking out and the cost of remaining silent. Values call you. They aren't always in you. As each step to be brave challenged me, so it called on me to understand who I was as a person, as a pastor. Not everything is a perfect fit; I was learning as I went.

■ ■ ■

Fortunately, my mentor and supervisor, Dan Ramm, saw my love for small-town ministry in the city and, knowing I had done a good job at Flatlands, suggested Greenpoint would be a good fit—even as it would be a real challenge.

Though not all that far from Flatlands, Greenpoint felt like a continent away. If you know New York City, you know it is a city of neighborhoods, and most residents can easily tell you the reason why their neighborhood is the best. Ask someone from Brooklyn about Queens, and they are likely to throw their hands in the air, frustrated by its quirky naming system for Streets, Avenues, Ways, and Drives. Ask someone from Manhattan about Staten Island, and they will know it as the place in New York City inhabited by lots of Republicans. Other than Yankee Stadium, nobody outside the Bronx really knows much about the Bronx. But poor Greenpoint was a neighborhood that was so far off the beaten path, very few people knew it even existed. As with most New York neighborhoods, Greenpoint has been occupied by several waves of immigrants, starting with the Dutch in the mid-1800s. In the beginning of the 20th century, it was an industrial neighborhood, peppered with manufacturing facilities and the Brooklyn Navy Yard. After World War II, the manufacturing exodus began, and with it, the workers left for the Long Island suburbs. There was a mini-boom in the 1980s when a wave of post-Solidarity Polish shipbuilders emigrated to take jobs at the navy yard. In fact, it's still known today as a Polish neighborhood—you can see Polish stores and signage on most of the major streets. When I arrived in 2003, Greenpoint—and especially the Greenpoint Reformed Church—had experienced a lot of decline. Which also meant that it might be due for a turnaround.

Greenpoint is directly across the East River from Midtown Manhattan, but it's perceived as isolated because it is blessed—or cursed—with being served by what is universally known as the worst subway line on the MTA, the G train. The G train has earned its reputation; it is unreliable, infrequent and crowded, and by virtue of being the only line that does not touch Manhattan, requires a change of trains for Greenpointers who work in Manhattan. Plus, the perception of the G train is that the schedules are . . . well, more like suggestions. If you miss a G train, you should expect to wait a long time for the next one. Could be ten minutes, could be twenty, could be a lifetime. Paradoxically, given that it's a relatively forgotten line, the trains tend to be very full. It's the only line that runs four-car trains. That means it's not enough to get down to the platform, you need to get to the middle of the platform, because the platforms are built for ten cars. You can always tell the G train newbies when it arrives because you will invariably see some tourist or Manhattan-ite running frantically down the platform when the train stops at what feels like a block away. You only have to make that mistake once to learn that waiting at the end of the platform is a recipe to either run like hell or miss the train.

If you rely on the G train, it can be hard to maintain a true Type A personality. This has helped keep Greenpoint real estate values lower than most of New York City and has made the community a lot more down-to-earth than the rest of Brooklyn. It also helped our congregation immensely; we didn't have to worry about keeping up with the Joneses. No Jones worth their weight in salt would ever deign to live in Greenpoint.

Maybe that isolation is the reason Dan thought Greenpoint Reformed Church was a perfect starting point for me, or perhaps even more likely—he loved that little congregation and he loved me too—he thought we might be a good match. Originally formed in 1848 by the Dutch immigrants of the community, at its peak the morning worship service would draw almost a thousand congregants. But because of the congregation's steady decline since the first half of the 20th century, by 2003 the church was held together by a handful of dedicated church folks.

As it turned out, Dan's former wife, Ann Akers, had been preaching as pulpit supply at Greenpoint Reformed, and they both knew that the church needed a permanent pastor. Only a few weeks after I left Flatlands, Dan and Ann connected me with Ruth Blankschen, one of the church's leaders, and we quickly booked a time for me to meet her. After an unusually short discussion, Ruth suggested that I preach at Greenpoint—*that Sunday.* It was a Thursday. My time at Flatlands had just concluded, so the date was open on my calendar. I took a deep breath and, in the spirit of Go Big, I said two important things.

First, I explained how heartbroken I was about Flatlands and how I didn't want that to happen again at Greenpoint. I was asking for a "promise of a call." That's where the church lets the seminarian know they'll call them to be pastor once seminary is over and they're eligible for ordination. I knew I was not the typical candidate, and I certainly didn't fit the stereotype of the seminarian who would demand that kind of commitment. Then my voice got kind of quiet and I said, "The other thing you need to know is that I am gay. And if it's going to be a problem for the congregation, that's totally understandable. But I don't want to keep it a secret from you. If we're going to work together, I want you to know who I really am. If that doesn't work for you, I fully understand."

Greenpoint had been without a pastor for a *long* time at this point. I don't think they thought anyone would *want* to receive a promise of a call from them because they didn't have enough money to pay for a full-time pastor. Ruth wasn't expecting me to want to "go steady" with Greenpoint—the congregation was used to getting turned down for dates to the prom. But I did. And she assured me there wouldn't be a problem with being out. We were both quite happy to have found a match for each other's needs. To top it off, the Greenpoint call came with housing, right upstairs.

This was a huge "Go Big or Go Home" moment. The big ask. Telling the truth of who I was. Putting it all on the line—my heartbreak, my hopes—and bringing my true self. I was a seminarian who had just been rejected by another congregation. Plus, I was a gay seminarian in a denomination that had been divided about how to deal with, in their words, "homosexual clergy." But here's the thing about kick-ass values: *you don't get to turn them on and off*. I couldn't say I was living by these values and then selectively decide *when* I was going to live by them.

That first Sunday I showed up with chocolate chip cookies for coffee time. The lessons of the cookie rating system of my youth were not lost on me: nothing smooths over the acceptance of a visitor like high-quality baked goods. I think we had eight people there for my "trial sermon." It was Transfiguration Sunday and the final hymn, one of my favorites, was "Blessed Assurance." I took that as a sign that this was meant to be and sang very joyfully. Later, over the cookies I left behind, those eight people gathered and asked each other, "Well, do you like her?" Everyone agreed they should call me.

I fell in love with the church at Greenpoint, which is to say, I fell in love with the matriarchs, the ones who kept the church going. We had three: Irene, Ruth (who was only forty-five so I'm not sure she officially qualified for matriarch status), and Grace, a public health nurse who came to the church in 1970 when the Methodist Church in her neighborhood closed. My first official day at Greenpoint, the congregation had declined to three congregants. I was given another gift that day: the gift of desperation. With all that had already happened with the church, there was little to fear in handing the reins over to a young lesbian. And when you're down to three congregants, you only have one way to go—up. I was going big.

ABSOLUTELY NOTHING SHOCKS GRACE

Honesty

Sometimes values build on each other, inform each other. You become authentic to yourself (or God holds up a Victoria's Secret mirror and helps you get authentic), then you take bigger steps to live a life and a calling. You get authentic with others. You go big. I didn't know what was next, but each value, each anchor that informed my next steps, was as challenging as it was freeing.

Jen and I hadn't been dating long when I started at Greenpoint, and on Christmas Eve of that year, I asked her to marry me. That's the thing about good Christian girls—we don't move in together, we get married. Around the same time, Massachusetts made gay marriage legal, so it felt like a bit of kismet. I didn't have a roadmap showing me how to manage this. Honestly, I wasn't really sure whether gay marriage was going to be legal in my lifetime, and I certainly wasn't obligated to discuss it with the church elders. But I knew it was a controversial issue and I felt obligated to be honest and up front about it. In fact, I'm probably the only minister I know who felt she needed to get permission from her consistory to get married.

First, I asked Grace. I was comfortable with her, and I thought she would be a good test case. She replied, "Oh! I didn't know you people wanted to get married," which initially turned me off a bit, until it became clear that by "you people" she meant young people. Irene was a different story. I was nervous asking her because part of her role in the congregation was to protect the church. It can take decades to build trust with a skeptical church matriarch, and Irene had lots of reasons to be skeptical. I had recently landed a donation of a washer/dryer, desperate as I was to not have to schlep over to the laundromat. But back in the 1980s someone had installed a washer in the parsonage and it had leaked—an epic leak. A *biblical leak*. Nothing could convince Irene that it would be safe to install this new machine. We went back and forth for weeks. Each time I'd try some new way of asking, and each time she'd say no. I was afraid, I will admit it, of Irene.

Honestly, I was intimidated by each of the matriarchs. In one of my early sermons, I mentioned I wasn't sure whether or not I believed in prayer. After the service we talked about it, and not only was I the answer to their prayers for a new energetic pastor, I was told, but I realized that they were living examples of how prayer worked. These women were fully committed. They showed up, no matter how bleak things looked. When Greenpoint drew just three people to a service, they never lost faith in the church's ability to recover. They prayed for it, they worked to make it happen, and they rejoiced in it. I came to realize that the power of the matriarchs was, and is, one of the most important forces in the church.

I knew that I needed their collective and individual blessings to feel comfortable with the marriage. I didn't know what Irene would say when I finally got up the courage to tell her about my plans to marry Jen. Jen was anxious too and waited for me to report back about it when I finally spoke to Irene. I returned without an answer. Somehow, we'd been interrupted and she never really gave me a yes. But she also didn't give me a no, and if it had been a no, she would have said so. I heard repeated "no's" every time I asked about the washer. That she never said no about this was the go-ahead I needed. We went forward with the wedding, and they all got invited. It was lovely. So much joy.

But it didn't take long for the controversy to erupt. Word spread. People voiced opinions. One minister in the denomination wrote an angry email titled, yes, "Put a Finger in the Dyke." I'm sure whoever wrote this thought the reference to the Dutch story of *Hans Brinker: Or, The Silver Skates* was brilliant and witty. Really, though, it was incredibly hurtful. I more or less freaked out. I was angry and disappointed and scared. I started doing a lot of emotional eating, gained weight, and just kind of sulked around, spending many sleepless nights on the internet searching for the latest thing someone had said.

Grace and Irene had to attend what seemed like endless RCA (Reformed Church of America) meetings about how their church had called a lesbian pastor. Both were incredibly gracious in having to listen to people say all kinds of ridiculous, hateful things about me. In one meeting, a particular pastor said the words "anal sex" at least three times. Each time, I blushed. I was *not* ready to have any conversations about sexuality, especially in a church context, and I attempted to apologize to Grace and Irene for his behavior. Grace's response was characteristic of her outlook on life: "Oh, honey, I was a public health nurse in New York City in the 1960s. Nothing can shock me." It was true—absolutely nothing shocked Grace.

My father, who had officiated our wedding, was surprisingly calm throughout. He felt called to the whole thing and was trusting in God's providence. I, on the other hand, preferred to have more control over the situation. But sometimes when you get authentic, when you go big or go home, and when you get honest, you don't get the value-add of *control*. Church, especially, is a prime environment for gossip and rumors and people sharing their unsolicited opinions. And the Reformed tradition I was in is rife with ministers who think they hold the one true doctrine.

Sociologically, the RCA is a mash-up of different groups of Dutch folks, and where two or three are gathered, there is likely to be argument and schism. Eastern congregations are more connected to the original Dutch settlers; churches are older, historic, and have a bit more of a trader's ethos: open to others, ecumenical. Many midwestern churches date back to an emigration in the mid-1800s and tend to be more conservative theologically, with a sense of religious autonomy from the liberalism of the Netherlands, where they sang songs other than Psalms. (Like hymns, believe it or not!) And in the West, you've got an ethos connected to the 1950s expansion and American evangelicalism. Robert Schuller, of the Crystal Cathedral, was a Reformed Church minister. Given the tensions within the RCA, issues of liberalism/modernism and ecumenism/purity are not new. But the issue of the day—or decade—still is, as they say, "homosexuality." And our wedding created a perfect storm.

In 2004, when Dad graciously agreed to officiate our wedding, he was still president of the New Brunswick Theological Seminary, one of two RCA seminaries in the country, and the first seminary in the United States. The fallout within the church was intense and immediate. Within six months he had lost his job as president of the seminary, and soon thereafter, a group of RCA ministers filed charges against him for heresy. Trials in the RCA are extremely rare—in fact, the only previous trial took place around the time of the founding of the seminary, in the mid-1700s.

My father's trial was held in upstate New York in June of 2005. Similar to a legal trial, there were lawyers, stacks of evidence (including our marriage license and the license my dad obtained from the Commonwealth of Massachusetts as an out-of-state officiant), fact witnesses. I myself was asked to testify, and confirm that yes, I did marry Jen, and yes, my dad did officiate. After the trial and deliberation, the ruling came down: by about a two-to-one margin, the synod ruled that my dad had broken church rules and committed heresy. He was dismissed and defrocked as a professor of theology. He was also suspended as a Minister of Word and Sacrament.

As we were exiting the meeting hall following my dad's trial, a fellow seminary classmate of mine approached me. He was also one of the ministers who had brought charges against my dad. He was about my age, and generally a sweet, angelic guy—he genuinely wanted to reconcile with me and was headed toward me with that intent. I pointed my finger at him and said, sternly, "Not now!" But he continued to approach me and somehow, magically, I balled up my fist and started swinging it in the direction of that gentleman's nose. This is the downside of practicing Go Big or Go Home values, but luckily for both of us, the Holy Spirit—in the form of my 6-foot-7-inch-tall brother—appeared. His arm shot out, like Inspector Gadget's, and grabbed my fist before I could make contact, saving both of us. Never before had the Lord (or my brother) worked such a miracle in my life, nor has the Lord ever done it again.

The day after the trial, our family and friends gathered for breakfast at the restaurant at the Holiday Inn Express in Schenectady. At the hostess stand was a stack of the *Albany Times-Union* and apparently, we were big news. The front page ran a picture of my dad and a headline about the trial in large type. It was a bit uncomfortable, but not much daunts my dad, especially when anticipating a free hotel breakfast. In this stressful situation, there was only one solution: we all needed free hash browns.

When we were seated as a group, we quickly started to stock up on comfort food. As it turns out, we were not alone in the restaurant. Right next to us was a prayer group of evangelical pastors who met in the restaurant every week. The ministers were excitedly discussing the topical issue of the day—my father's trial. They were in full agreement with the synod, and compared notes on the "evils of homosexuality," gay marriage, and miscreant ministers.

Then, as ministerial prayer groups are wont to do, they started to pray. Loudly. About how terrible my father was, and how thankful they were to be so right in the gospel. Enraged and eager to finish the work that the Lord and my brother stopped earlier, I pushed my chair back, ready to nose-flat the pastors. In that moment, my dad said to me, "Annie, go to your room," and that's exactly what I did. I got up and walked right out. When my dad started a command with "Annie" I knew it was serious. I made it all the way to the second floor, got to the door and took my keycard out, then I stopped. *Why did I come to my room?* I thought. *I'm not a child anymore.* I turned around and headed back to the restaurant.

It was like a bomb had gone off in my absence. My dad was at the pastors' table introducing himself. "Hello, I am Norman Kansfield, and you have been praying about me." Imagine the surprise among the pastors. I can only guess that they were cursing their luck, or lack thereof, to be seated right next to the heretical Rev. Kansfield. It would have been easy—and understandable—for my dad to let these pastors stew in their opinions of him. But my dad knew that honesty required that he acknowledge his accusers and talk with them. He dove right in: "I've been listening to you pray, and do you realize that you are being like the Pharisees, praying so righteously that you are not like me? Well, I just wanted to introduce myself to you."

It was such a "Go Big, Be Honest" moment for him. I stood beside my dad. I didn't think I would change their minds. I knew they wouldn't change mine. Many of us have the tendency to think, "I'm right, I'm the righteous one. I tithe ten percent, I'm so holy. Thank you, God, for not making me like *them*." When we hear people talk about other folks being beyond God's grasp, we don't think that's about us, that we're the ones less fortunate. I don't know what those pastors thought when my dad came to talk to them. I don't know what they said the following week when they met in our absence. But I hope my dad accomplished one thing: make them pause long enough to consider who gets to bask in God's love.

That breakfast was the culmination of a difficult experience for my dad. He was a theologian and an educator, and the trial meant that he could no longer be either of those, at least not in an official capacity. But for him, no matter how upset he was, he always thought of himself as a pastor first. His job was to share God's love with everyone, whether he agreed with them or not. To be honest and speak honestly. Those are callings and values—true God Code—I'll never forget.

At the time, in my mind, my dad's trial felt almost like the worst-case scenario. I feared his own values, his loyalty to me, and his adherence to the honesty in his own God Code had led him to lose what he valued most. And it was all my fault. Yet, it allowed me to conquer my fears and look to the future. Honesty can do that. And sometimes, what happens as a result of your honesty is reflected in the well-known teaching by the 17th-century Japanese poet and samurai Mizuta Masahide: *The barn burned down. Now I can see the moon.*

■ ■ ■

As hard as that experience was for my dad, things in Greenpoint were looking up. The church had started to grow. One Sunday, two or three families with kids showed up, all at the same time. At Greenpoint Reformed Church, that was a miracle! Not only did they show up, they stuck around. At the same time, we started to see more of our impact in the neighborhood. I knew that bringing a new gay pastor and her wife into a moribund church was going to be a *story* in a small community like Greenpoint. What I didn't anticipate was all the positive response.

One morning a neighbor from across the street rang the doorbell of the church. I hadn't ever spoken to her before. "Pastor Ann," she said, "I just wanted to come over here and tell you how thankful we are that you and your wife live here and are at this church." It was an amazing gift. Another bit of support came from a Catholic priest who invited me to preach on one of the days of the Easter Triduum. For a non-Catholic to preach at a Catholic church, and within the focused time of a liturgical season, is, well, let's just say it's not done. I thought he must have been sleeping under a rock to have missed the story about my dad being fired for officiating at my homosexual wedding. And for anyone reading this who might hail from the hierarchy of the Catholic Church, I'm confident he had no idea. But as people exited the sanctuary after the service, a very sweet older woman whispered in my ear, "We all read the article about you in *The Greenline* (the local paper) and we're cheering you on." And consistent with my cookie rating system and what constitutes a good church, there was tea and a stellar supply of baked goods after church.

It wasn't all smooth. My dad's trial became national news and, of course, most of the articles mentioned

Greenpoint, so I became neighborhood-famous. The story was all over the TV and newspapers. I wanted to barf I was so upset. One of the women from another local church called Irene, saying, "Did you know your pastor is on the television?"

Irene responded, "Yes."

"Oh," said the other church lady. "Oh, I just thought that maybe *you would want to know*. And you knew about her wedding?"

Irene said, "Yes, we knew about the wedding. We were invited."

With that, the busybody church lady said, "Oh well, then. Goodbye."

Greatest church lady gossip shutdown ever.

And then there was the hate mail. One of the guys in our congregation offered to answer some of the hate mail that came in to the church's email account. I thanked him, because I was having a hard time with it. When I asked him what he was going to say in his response, he said, "I'm going to say, 'You may be right.'" I wasn't sure about that response at first, but within a few seconds I realized it was brilliant. They may be right. I may be going to hell. And then he added, "But we disagree with you."

Around this time, I developed what I call the "Ten Block Rule." I could easily lose my focus and start worrying about who was doing what in the denomination.

So, to keep me from freaking out and going down that rabbit hole, I told myself if it didn't happen within a ten-block radius of the church, it wasn't my problem and I wasn't allowed to worry about it. (Sometimes "Go Small and Be Home" is a helpful additional principle.) It helped me to remember we were on the G train. When I'd worry that someone would try to get me removed or we'd get some emotionally charged piece of hate mail, I'd remind myself that Greenpoint was on the G train and *no one* takes the G train anywhere.

Even the support and love were sometimes uncomfortable for me. I was freaking out inside because I still had so much internalized homophobia. I wondered if my dad deserved what happened to him: he broke the rules and he made a scene in the church. Now it felt like everyone was mad at both of us, and obviously I deserved it because I was gay and had the audacity to actually marry Jen.

One of the big things that helped me move past my fears was finding an honest way to remain connected to my RCA roots while also being differentiated. I could have cut and run and told them to screw themselves. But in my heart I loved the RCA. These were my people; the denomination had so many wonderful ones. Even the ones who disagreed with my dad and put him on trial were still "my people." They might have wanted us out, and I certainly was ready to do some nose-crushings in the moment, but I also wanted to stay connected in a way that honored who I was, was honest about who I was. I had to learn to accept and not be afraid of the harsh voices and homophobic critics—to see them as humans, just like my dad saw those pastors at the Holiday Inn Express.

Over a decade later, I had an encounter with a pastor who was the president of the General Synod during my dad's trial. I didn't know him, but we were at the same retreat together. When I first saw him there, every fiber in my body wanted to run away. But I prayed and centered myself and eventually we ended up talking, and not just fake chitchat. We talked openly and honestly about our experience at the trial. It turned out, I had no idea what was going on with him, and he didn't know what was going on with me. It took each of us honestly pushing past our fears to connect. When we did, we realized that learning what the other person was going through in that very emotionally charged moment was extremely healing. There was a deep connection, a wholeness.

Thinking about my life's journey so far, I realize that the God Code contained all the tools I needed to complete it. Authenticity got me off of Wall Street and brought me to seminary. Going big brought me to congregational ministry and led me to Greenpoint. And honesty helped me to make sure I was living my values wholeheartedly. Adhering to these values wasn't always easy. Both as a pastor of our little congregation and as a human out in the world, it took a lot to move beyond fear, to trust that I was okay. But over time, I began to trust that the values were enough. I was enough. God was enough.

As the dust settled in Greenpoint, Jen and I got back to being pastors. We ministered while she finished seminary, and our little church started to grow. Officially, I worked part-time at the church. The "pay package" didn't exactly represent the amount of work that was needed. As Jen graduated from seminary, we proposed to the consistory that she and I work as co-pastors at the church. It was really a great deal—two for the price of one! Or, as I like to joke, "our church really needed two pastors *and* two pastors' wives."

I didn't realize it at the time, but we were about to meet the biggest week of our lives, which certainly didn't feel big at all in the moments proceeding it—we had no idea what we were getting ourselves into. In one week, we would start a Hunger Program in Greenpoint and Jen would be ordained. And apparently, as we sat in a circle with other pastors for the laying on of hands ceremony, Jen felt lightheaded and realized that she was pregnant. We were about to expand our definition of Go Big.

5

BE THE BRAVE ONE

Courage

One of my jobs is chaplain for the New York City Fire Department, or as it's better known, the FDNY. I wasn't a natural choice to become a chaplain, but I think I was actually preordained, so to speak. My grandfather, a firefighter, died when I was a freshman in high school. At his funeral, someone noted in a eulogy that the three most important things in his life were his family, the fire department, and the church—in that order. I was slightly concerned that the fire department outranked the church and that perhaps God might not be so pleased about that. Now, I can see how the fire service could be easier to love than the church. The two have a lot of similarities: groups of people living out a calling.

A very distinctive part of visiting my grandfather's house was the phone ringing and him answering,

"Hello," and then not saying anything for a few seconds before hanging up. Even though he had retired, the fire department kept him on their callout list. He'd hang up the phone, then say, "Fire call," and if my dad or aunt were around, he might fill in a detail or two about the location of the emergency. During one of my last visits, there was a fire at the local hospital. A patient receiving oxygen had insisted on smoking in bed. That evening, as the family gathered for dinner, an impromptu incident debriefing took place. My aunt and her daughter-in-law worked as nurses at the hospital. My cousin worked as a firefighter for a neighboring department. Each of them had been involved in the situation. As I listened in on their conversation, I became keenly aware that many members of my family did life-and-death work. It sounded exciting and important—even more exciting than a television drama.

I didn't know about the concept of chaplains in the fire service until 9/11. But in the days and weeks following that fateful Tuesday, I learned about Father Mychal Judge, an FDNY chaplain who died at Ground Zero. Instantaneously, Father Judge became a role model for me. His love of people and of the city is legendary. I thought: *that would be a really cool job for me.*

But as with most of life's big dreams, there's a big distance between thinking about it and actually *doing* it. I had a long way to go. Whenever I met someone who might have information or wisdom about the job, though, I would ask them. It became clear that there weren't many opportunities to land the job and that, for the most part, it would probably depend on having some political connections.

A few years later, I was at a field education "job fair" at Union Theological Seminary attempting to recruit a seminarian to work at our church. A few tables down from me was Father Chris Keenan, who worked as a—you guessed it—fire department chaplain. I was excited to meet him. We talked for a long time, and after the event concluded, he offered me a ride in his totally amazing vehicle with lots of fancy-looking fire department radios. (In reality, it was probably an almost-over-the-hill Crown Victoria with well over 100,000 miles on it, but that did not take away from my sense of thinking it was super cool.) I came home excited to tell Jen all about my afternoon with this real-life fire chaplain. What impressed us both about my detailed report was that I ended it by saying, "Well, I should plan on waiting at least another twenty years before even thinking of doing that job, because I'm going to need to be a lot more spiritually mature to do that work. I'm a little fish right now and should swim in the lake for a while so I can grow into being a keeper."

Two or three years went by—far less time than I had imagined—and I was part of a Facebook group for young clergywomen who asked one another questions and offered suggestions on a wide variety of ministry-related things. A local colleague posted asking if anyone had ever worked as a fire chaplain. One of her congregants worked for the department and suggested that she consider applying for a new open position they had for a chaplain. My first instinct was to roar like a lion, *Step away from my job!* Clearly, I had some feelings, and thankfully I toned them down before I typed anything on the keyboard. It turned out that my colleague didn't feel called to the job. In retrospect, she shared with me that she could see how much I felt called to the work and she was excited to help me prepare for the interview process. If it hadn't been for her, I might have missed that the department was hiring. A terrifying thought for me.

I hadn't put together a résumé in over a decade. As a striver, it used to be almost an obsession for me to think about various activities and successes as "résumé builders." But once I started at Greenpoint, I felt content to the point that I wasn't looking to land a bigger, more shiny job. I did the things I felt God calling me to do and didn't think much about how they might look to the outside world. So, it took a bit of thinking to actually put together a résumé. Even more complicated was figuring out how to upload the résumé to the city website.

For several months, I didn't hear anything. Nonetheless, I reached out to everyone I knew who might have a connection with the fire department. And then an email arrived telling me to show up for an interview. In retrospect, I wonder if they gave me the interview merely to stop the deluge of calls they were getting about my interest in the job.

I met with several of the current chaplains and it seemed to go well, but deep down inside I still had some concerns about not being spiritually mature enough for the job. And then I waited again. Another month went by, and I received a call from a woman on behalf of the fire commissioner who wanted to schedule an interview with me. I could not contain my surprise and joy when he told me at the end of the interview that I got the job.

My time in the FDNY deepened my sense of calling. It's also helped me develop more of a sense of my values, my God Code. One day, talking with an old grizzled chief about why the firefighters of the FDNY are known as "New York's Bravest," he said, "We go in as a team. And that's where we find our courage. From one another. Really, only one of us has to be brave at any given time, and the rest will believe it and follow. But the secret is that none of us know which one of us is supposed to be the brave one at any given time." Hearing that, I knew that bravery would become another anchor value for me. I thought about how that had manifested for Jen, and for me and my father, and for the matriarchs of our church and others who withstood storms. Even the G train seemed to take on a new, brave, singular role.

Once you take on bravery as an anchor value, you start to see it in others. I think the best example in recent times has been the reaction of first responders to the COVID-19 virus. While most of us were self-isolating in our homes, countless first responders were reporting to work every day, making sure we could all receive medical treatment, buy food at a grocery store, get our mail, or ride the public transit system. I would guess that very few of those folks had ever imagined a crisis as bad as COVID-19, nor did any of them imagine the depths of the risk they would undertake just going to work in a pandemic. However, they showed up because of the collective will of the institutions: the hospitals, the police departments, the grocery stores, and the individuals who recognized their work as part of a much bigger task. And like the firefighters, when they were interviewed about bravery, they deflected. They didn't think they were being brave as individuals, but the amalgamation of these individuals created a brave front—brave enough to keep going back, day after day, when we didn't know if the pandemic would ever end.

You don't feel the burden of being the brave one all the time. But you *do* have faith that one of you will be brave, and that once someone sets the tone for bravery, the rest of you will follow. It actually takes pressure off the individual and transfers it to the larger team, and when the team starts to demonstrate courage, it translates back to individual courage. Courage is one of the foundations that supports us living out all our values. It takes courage to do the big things in life—an idea that would take on a life of its own, I would soon discover.

■ ■ ■

In the summer of 2007, the congregation at Greenpoint was in full-on conversation about the needs of our neighborhood. The Greenpoint Reformed Church Hunger Program didn't appear out of nowhere. We started the Hunger Program after receiving a $20,000 donation from an anonymous donor who had stipulated that it wasn't for religious purposes but was to serve the community. It just happened that the Bible lessons on the following two Sundays involved the story of the Good Samaritan, which asks, "Who is my neighbor?" and the story of Jesus sending disciples out, two by two, into the community. Jen preached a brilliant and inspiring sermon about this, after which the congregation figured the best way to move forward was to try to follow Jesus's instructions by going out and asking questions of our neighbors. We traversed the neighborhood, learned more about who our neighbors were, and then came back to talk about the best way to be a neighbor.

We learned that there were three main areas needing attention: immediate needs for people who were hungry, support for local artists (who, like all artists, were at risk of gentrification), and affordable housing. After that meeting, the congregation decided to form working groups to figure out what kind of actions we could take. First, we would take half the money and put in new lighting and create an art gallery. And the other half was startup funding for the Hunger Program. The concept of a hunger program was magnetic to me. In our family, my grandfather established a tradition of taking people out for food when they asked. In Greenpoint, there was no shortage of hungry people, and many of them knocked on our door asking for food. I found myself buying a lot of pizza for a lot of neighbors, to the point where it felt like feeding people had become an informal part of my service to Greenpoint, so I was especially happy when the congregation chose to make it a formal part of our ministry.

We formed a small task force to figure out how to address the immediate need of hunger in the neighborhood and discovered that everyone in the group except one person had needed some sort of food help at one time or another in their life. This helped us understand the need on a more personal level. From the first, the team set out to create a program designed to meet the kind of needs they themselves had experienced.

As it happened, there was a lot of turmoil in our personal lives. The last Sunday in April of 2008, my parents were in a head-on collision with a tanker truck and we weren't sure if they were dead or alive. When we got to the hospital, we learned that they were going to make it, but my dad was in really bad shape. On Wednesday morning of that week, Jen got up to go to Brooklyn to handle the food pantry, and she called to tell me there were so many people waiting that our small front yard was already packed. She gave out the last of the food. While Jen is an ordained minister, unfortunately she was unable to immediately duplicate Jesus's skills with loaves and fish. We were out of food. Jen also told me that the church had no money to purchase more and that I would "need to figure it out and do something."

In the spirit of being the brave one and knowing that someone on the team can be brave for you or believe for you until you can be brave yourself, I made a call to one of the matriarchs. Irene, unflappable, told me she would pray. I whispered a thin "Help," grateful she would carry this. Jen's call, combined with having been with my parents in the hospital since the accident, gave me a brilliant idea. (Actually, a second brilliant idea, after calling Irene.)

There had been a huge outpouring of love for my dad from the RCA after his car accident. Kind of like an "Oh shit, we might not have done right by Norm, but we certainly didn't want him to *die*." In the middle of that night, as if from a vision (thank you, Irene) I realized I could send a giant email to all my dad's friends, tell them about the accident and ask for donations to the Hunger Program in lieu of flowers. I ran the idea by my dad, which, okay, I'll admit wasn't really fair since he was pretty out of it on pain meds. But I was like, "Hey, Dad, I need to use your accident to buy some food for the pantry. Would that be okay? You don't really need flowers anyway, so wouldn't you rather get money for hungry people? Yeah. Okay. I'll make that happen for you, Dad."

And that's how we bridged the gap with the pantry. We had to be in operation for more than six months before the Food Bank would take us on as a member agency, and until that happened, we were not eligible for any other food aid. We couldn't join City Harvest, couldn't get access to government food, or any of the formal programs that help the food pantries of New York City. The money I raised, literally off my dad's back, carried us for another two months. By that point we were just shy of qualifying and still needed another

$1,000 for food. Irene and the matriarchs still praying, I got desperate and called the RCA home office. I wasn't sure they would send us any money, since we were definitely persona non grata (or ecclesia non grata, as the case may be). But they sent us about $1,000 from the One Great Hour of Sharing offering that was collected to be distributed to pantries. It was a miracle.

The first week of the program, we had planned for about twenty people to attend. By spring, we had one hundred people coming for groceries and dinner. Jen's pregnancy progressed as the Hunger Program grew, and I was simultaneously balancing my job that made money to pay for my preaching habit, and my job as pastor to a growing congregation with a new hunger program. To top it all off, a newborn was about to be added to the mix. (Given my short-lived time as a Sunday School teacher, that probably scared me more than any of the other challenges.)

Unfortunately, the economy started to turn into recession just as I was hoping to take family leave from that money-making job. Surprisingly, or perhaps not so surprisingly, instead of family leave, my boss gave me an unlimited leave. They decided they didn't actually need me and that an administrative assistant could do my work and save them money. I didn't see this coming, and I remember calling Jen to tell her the surprising, kind of embarrassing, news that I had lost my job just weeks before the baby was due. She responded, "I guess I really did marry you for richer or for poorer. We'll figure it out."

My own code was still coming together. I knew that authenticity had gotten me to ministry. Going big led me to this congregation. Honesty, to myself and to my community, had helped me fulfill a vision while staying true to myself. And even considering creating a hunger program, from scratch, and with a relatively small nest egg, was the epitome of bravery. But I counted on the safety net of that other money-making job to keep us fed and clothed. Not only was bravery vital, it was a requirement!

The rapid growth of the Hunger Program was difficult to balance. As scary as it was to lose my job, it helped me realize that we could scale the program bigger if I could devote more time to the effort. The economy continued to get worse, and more people were coming to us for food. We decided to offer two programs: a weekly dinner service and a food bank, or pantry, so our guests could get food on the other six days of the week. Although food was at the core of both programs, the logistics of the two were quite different. Even tougher, we faced a unique challenge: most of our guests were Polish, with limited English skills and lots of cultural differences. It was difficult to communicate the necessity of following directions, and they'd line up earlier and earlier every day. The lines and the noise pissed off some of our neighbors on the block, and there were constant fights among our guests about who had which place in line. It was like Polish granny wars on the front lawn.

Several neighbors on the block were angry about guys they perceived as homeless coming for dinner, and they were frustrated that the pantry line would extend out the gate and down the block. We worked hard to appease their anger, but there was nothing we could do that would actually satisfy them. One neighbor knocked on the door and said, "This used to be a quiet church with a pretty little garden, and now look at the filth you are bringing onto our block. These are million-dollar brownstones we're talking about." She did have a point. We *did* used to be a quiet church with a pretty garden. When we had dropped to eight members, one of the eight was a professional gardener, and he had the yard landscaped beautifully. Sure, the front gate was padlocked except for a few hours a week, but the garden was beautiful.

We also had some great neighbors who were support-ive of the mission. There's a Broadway show called *Come from Away*, which is the true story of what happened on September 11, when dozens of planes were diverted to Newfoundland into a small community that was completely unprepared to feed and house thousands of people. In it, there's a scene where a guy from Brooklyn is told to borrow a bunch of propane grills from various neighbors' backyards in Gander, Newfoundland. Understandably, he fears that if someone sees him, they'll assume he's stealing and might shoot him. When I heard that line, I laughed out loud—that was a uniquely Brooklyn experience. It's impossible to find propane in Brooklyn, and I'm not gonna lie, I have temporarily liberated a propane tank when the Hunger Program was in dire need, yelling over my shoulder, "It's okay, the Lord has need of a little propane!" The good news is that our neighbors were good sports. In fact, when one moved out of their place, they left me two full tanks of propane!

To a degree, I did empathize with the neighbors. Change is hard. They were used to the way things were. Greenpoint was a sleepy neighborhood and they weren't happy with this type of change. But part of me thought, *I know it was a dormant church, but it's like buying a home near an unused railroad track. You have to know that there is a chance that things are going to change.* In this case, my opinion was, you should always be aware that at any time a church might start doing Jesus-like things and then all heaven can break loose. The way I saw it, it was not my fault—blame Jesus! Any Bible reader out there had to realize Jesus's propensity for showing up and feeding people.

Another neighbor of ours had a habit of consuming a few drinks himself and then coming over to yell at me about drunk homeless guys relieving themselves on his lawn. Our guests never scared me, but he did. He would get in my face and scream at me with alcohol-infused spittle filling the space between us. It would make me anxious, to the point where I begged our guests not to congregate on Milton Street, except for dinner, because the neighbors were so hostile. I regret saying that; I fear it might have suggested to our guests that I was embarrassed by them. That was not the case, of course. I just wanted the neighbors to stop yelling at me.

The Food Bank—the city's non-profit organization that delivered our food—could also be a challenge. As a non-profit ourselves, I knew to not complain, but sometimes they didn't deliver the food when they were supposed to. Other times, they would drop off huge quantities when we didn't expect it and couldn't store it. It wasn't like ordering from Amazon. I'd place an order on Thursday and ask for it to be delivered the following Wednesday. They would call on Friday to confirm, but if I didn't pick up the phone, they'd cancel the order. And forget calling them back—sometimes *they* wouldn't answer the phone. We were on a tightrope without a net. Food Bank was also at the mercy of the organizations that donated food to them. Our food options were heavily dependent on the crop each year. Good year for corn farmers? Then we'd have lots of corn. We tried to market the crop the best way we knew. Corn is easy to push in a place like Greenpoint, but one year we got so much that even the guests pushed back.

Starting the hunger ministry was the most stressful and, dare I say, brave/foolish thing I had ever done. The day-to-day management required every last bit of brain power and skill and muscle we had. It goes without saying that for a Hunger Program, there's nothing worse than running out of food, and this was especially stressful for our client base, since so many of them had experienced breadlines and rations during the Cold War. Running out of food was a familiar experience for them, sometimes leading to panic. But, good news, our guests knew *exactly* what to do in that situation: they would line up earlier and earlier in the day to make sure they were able to eat before the food ran out. And you already know how much the neighbors loved that.

We were in a state of low-grade panic. We needed to address this unforeseen success somehow. The first plan was to spread the demand. Originally, we ran both a food pantry and a dinner program on Wednesday afternoons, so we moved the food pantry to Thursdays from three to five p.m. As it turns out, we had trained our guests very well. If the program started at three, they arrived at two. When the line was long at two, they arrived at one. Trying to mitigate the disruption with the neighbors, we spread it out from one to five p.m. Then eleven to five. We eventually moved the start time all the way back to nine a.m. No matter the time, we were always greeted with a line. One day, I talked to a guy who had arrived at five a.m. to get the best spot among the Polish grannies, who then tried to sweet talk *their* way into a better spot in the line.

Second, we needed to simplify the process. Wanting to give people as much choice as possible, we offered a few different types of cereal, beverages, or canned vegetables. But we discovered that when they got to the front of the line, having choices only added to our guests' agitation. To them, it seemed we were offering two things and then taking away one. So, we reduced the choices—less stress for them, and it also helped speed up the process. It made a difference, when, at one point, we were serving around two hundred people per week. It felt herculean.

During this time, Jen and I read a book called *Take this Bread* by Sara Miles. It was about her experience starting a food pantry in San Francisco and had inspired us to visit that city on our next vacation. (I had never been there, and Jen was so horrified she threatened to revoke my lesbian membership card.) The only thing I really wanted to see was Sara's food pantry. When we met her and she showed us around, we immediately envied the amount of space Sara had in her beautiful church. Greenpoint was on a standard New York City lot—fifty feet wide by one hundred feet deep. Sara's pantry was serving about six hundred people at the time, an unimaginably huge number to us. But we were comforted to learn she had many of the same challenges we did. And when she nonchalantly said, "When you get to the point where you're serving four hundred people," we just laughed. I couldn't even imagine serving that many people. Sure enough, within a year of the visit, we had doubled in size, and eventually we were serving seven hundred people a week. Between the relentless pressure from the neighbors, the continual fear of letting down our guests, and the fact that our internal processes were not equipped to handle this many people, we realized it was not sustainable. And we had no idea how to fix it.

The matriarchs prayed. In response, God gave us Christine. Frankly, there is no story of the Hunger Program without Christine. She personified the value of being the brave one. Christine became the queen of the kitchen, the "head chef"—both in title and in function. To call her colorful is to do a disservice to the word. Christine was tall, with long blonde hair and perfect lipstick. She was a true artist—creative in every way. She made a living restoring art for a wide range of exciting clients. She could mend a hole in a canvas or repair paint that might have gotten dinged by an overly zealous mover. She lived on the block and had a studio in the old Eberhard Faber Pencil Factory building. Christine grew up on Long Island and had the accent to prove it. The whole church would light up with energy and excitement whenever she crossed the threshold. Occasionally, Christine would nonchalantly drop a famous name in the context of a conversation, but never in a way that felt fake or forced. She didn't do it to prove she was cool. Exactly the opposite—she invited you into the action of the story so you would feel cool too. She hung out in the early days of the music scene at CBGBs and went to art school with Keith Haring. These were her friends, and everyone wanted to be Christine's friend.

This queen of the kitchen was no Queen Elizabeth, smiling, waving, and holding a corgi. She was more Catherine the Great, ruling with an iron fist, always loving but definitely in charge. Volunteers would come and go, but she had a cadre of her own that showed up religiously and kept the engine running. As the program grew, Christine found a way to make it work—always turning out delicious food cooked with love. There may have been some momentary freakouts about not enough volunteers or ingredients or disposable aluminum pans, but she made it work. It's like the old Lorne Michaels line about *Saturday Night Live*: the show doesn't go on because it's ready, the show goes on because it's eleven-thirty, or in our case, the meal went out at six p.m.

Christine was a bit of a freelancer, and that put us in tough positions with our guests. If someone asked for extra, or came on other days of the week, Christine would sneak them food. I understood why, but it created tension with the volunteers: she would say yes after they said no. I was ecstatic that the program flexed up as the demand increased, but observing the kitchen scared me to death. Christine was the only one who knew where everything was, and she had—at best—a *very* loose acquaintance with the concept of food safety and, sometimes, inadvertently, without realizing it, may have made a cutting comment or two that might have intimidated a thinner-skinned volunteer. Then she would complain that she didn't have enough volunteers. She'd get frustrated and threaten to quit, which also scared me to death, but she was drawn to the chaos and the energy and the desire to always give out of abundance. "We have to feed the people!" she would say. Then she'd lower her voice and say it again: "Feed the people!"

Christine wasn't just queen of the kitchen; she was a beautiful friend. Being in her presence made me happy—even when she was anxious and sharp-tongued, she was someone I wanted to be around. She was a spark plug of electricity, a character, and most importantly, she loved people. Christine had a strong spirituality. Growing up Roman Catholic, she made her First Communion, but when she went to confession the following week, she mangled the prayers. The priest slammed the Bible down and told her not to come back until she could get the words right. She never again went to confession, and therefore, never again received communion in the Roman Catholic Church. She shared this with me not long after she had started cooking at the church. She asked me if we did confession at our church. I explained that yes, we do confession, but we do it all together during the Sunday worship service, not individually with a priest. "Protestants are really into efficiency—we take our sins directly to God," I said. "And you don't need a clergy person to forgive you. God does that. All I do is remind the congregation that they are forgiven." She thought that was a good idea. A few weeks later, she came to worship on Sunday morning, joined in the prayer of confession, and received the Eucharist. I was moved that someone who had been away for forty years was now coming back to Jesus—right there on Milton Street, right inside our little church.

Several years later, seemingly out of the blue, Christine took her life. I never understood why. If I had gotten a call that Christine was over at the 94th Precinct charged with murder, it would have made more sense to me than this. And I would have said, whoever it was must have had it coming to them, then I would have gladly bailed her out. That's not what happened. She was, indeed, going through a difficult time in her life. She shared about her depression. The soup kitchen seemed to be stressing her out. She didn't want to, but I had to make the tough call and suggest she take a break from cooking—not a permanent one, just long enough to lower her stress.

I know that she had reached out for professional help. She texted me not long before she died to say that she was feeling better and looking forward to coming back. She took a cross-country motorcycle trip with her husband and texted me a photo of herself wearing a leather jacket at one of the national parks. She died in California. A woman I had never met, but whose name I knew because she featured prominently in many of Christine's stories, called to tell us the news. I think she thought we already knew. I collapsed on the floor as I realized what she was telling me.

Christine's husband said she was on new medication, and one of the side effects was suicidal thoughts. Is that what happened? Only God knows. You can imagine the impact her death had on us, on the program. Her posse was devastated. Even the people she yelled at were weepy. Her departure was a deep tragedy. For months, maybe even a year, the food at the dinner totally sucked. It was as if the empty space left by her death needed to be grieved with shitty meatloaf and soggy veggies.

We never created solid processes and procedures— Christine didn't want or need them. It was all in her head; the rest of us were just along for the ride. In her absence, morale dropped, volunteers dribbled away, and the food tasted worse. Even so, more people were coming to us for food than ever before. On a typical Thursday, we'd have seven hundred people at the pantry. Sometimes, the line went down the block and around the corner. It felt like we were giving out food, rapid fire. We didn't have time to do it with much love or care. We hired a seminarian to help manage the program and made some changes, including reducing the number of times people could come to the pantry program from weekly to monthly. Things got slightly better, but we needed to make a bigger, braver decision.

We shut the program down during the summer of 2016 to perform the reset we sorely needed. We cleaned the kitchen from top to bottom, visited other kitchens to learn best practices, and drafted formal guidelines for volunteers. We made diagrams for how the physical space would operate—from the flow of receiving food to the process for distributing it. And when the program reopened two months later, though we had lost some guests, we quickly built back a more successful and organized program.

This structure has helped us offer a crucial resource to our neighbors in Greenpoint, and frankly, without this level of organization, we would have never been prepared for the influx of need as the COVID-19 pandemic washed over our beloved city in the spring of 2020. At the core, Greenpoint is still, in many ways, a working-class neighborhood, and given that COVID caused thousands of layoffs in industries like theater, bars and restaurants, travel, and retail, we were flooded with new clients at the exact time when our own practices needed to change, given the threat of the virus. Moreover, our volunteers had never signed up to be essential workers. However, like other first responders in that troubled time, they stepped up. The foundation that we developed with the reorganization allowed us to pivot and protect both our guests and our volunteers. The Wednesday night dinner went from a community meal to an individual takeout. We created prepackaged bags of food for our new pantry guests. We were able to serve many more of our neighbors, safely and efficiently.

Like most acts of bravery, we never expected this one to end the way it did. Courage, being the brave one, those values don't develop in a vacuum—they're forged in the heat of adversity, fear, and despair. These anchor values were holding me steady through some of the worst, and truly exciting, storms I'd ever navigated. Losing Christine felt like the bottom dropping out of our boat, one we'd worked so hard to get up and running. Even now, not a week goes by that I don't think about her and what she meant to the effort to end hunger in Greenpoint.

And if I ever do forget, our little stretch of Milton Street has been given the ceremonial name *Christine Zounek Way*, and I walk past the sign every day, thanking God that I was one of the lucky ones who experienced the gift of her friendship.

HOLIEST
SHIT HAPPENS

Acceptance

So, you may have noticed that I don't get *too* theological in this book, but I'm part of a faith tradition that has some wildly unpopular beliefs, even within its own tradition. For instance, Calvinist theology holds to the doctrine of original sin. Everyone, the worldview goes, is fundamentally flawed, starting with Adam and Eve. Let's just say the Calvinists are not always the most fun folks at parties.

One time, as an icebreaker at a church event in Orlando, the leaders asked people to stand up if they agreed with various beliefs of the church. They went through a list, most of which were light or interesting. When they asked people to stand up if they believed in "total depravity," four people stood up in a group of over a thousand: Abby (a friend from seminary), me, and two others. Abby and I looked at each other in surprise. In the bedrock of the Reformed tradition, we were probably among the most progressive in the group. That night, after the event, we went to the local Michael's craft store and bought materials to make ourselves T-shirts that said "Stand Up for Total Depravity."

When I hear someone say, "I'm a good person," I think, *I'm not good at all. I'm a total asshole. Any good that might possibly come from me is God's light shining through my ass-holey-nature.* When I die, and someone is preparing my eulogy, I hope they say, "That Ann, she was a total asshole for Jesus."

■ ■ ■

Muck starts early. Think of parenting. There is the normal element that all parents expect: the diapers, the puking, the regular food-throwing messes, and, of course, the potty training. Our son, John, was born in 2008, and we learned quickly that having a child is a seminal event when it comes to introducing muck into your life. But the real surprise for parents comes in those little unexpected moments of muck.

As the pastor of a church, I have learned that there is also a lot of muck and poop in ministry. Mostly metaphorical, but also legit, literal *shit.* If you saw *Forrest Gump*, you're familiar with the line "Shit happens."

Well, it *really* happens to ministers. We all have stories about some ecclesiastical baptism of fire that invariably includes shit. Parents among us know the book *Everyone Poops* by the Japanese author Taro Gomi. (If you're not a parent, stay with me here.) This book fulfills a vital role. Children think potty talk is spicy and salacious, and they aren't shy about using it, which usually gets a rise out of the adults. While the book demystifies "pooping," it's also meant to remove the word as a weapon in the child's shock-and-awe vocabulary. I'm not sure it works, but it gets people's attention.

So, call this chapter the mid-book poop jolt. The shock isn't the value anchor; dealing with muck and shit is. Whether you are the Pope, the president, or the guy who empties the trash cans on the G train, you share some core elements of humanity. And, well, everyone poops. Truly acknowledging that is a kind of rite of passage for faith leaders. I like to call it the Shit Story. New or old, every faith leader will have at least one memorable, uncomfortable interaction with the basest form of human excrement. I'm unlucky enough to have more than one.

To this day, I have no idea who left the human excrement in the basement of our church. Someone told me a sewage pipe had burst, and as I headed down the steps, I could smell what they were talking about before I could see it. It wasn't a burst pipe. A person had experienced some sort of explosive decompression in the basement and it had splattered across the floor and walls. I didn't know who did it, but I did know that in a small congregation like ours there was only one person who was going to clean up the shit: the pastor. In the world of shit assignments, this was the pinnacle. I bucked up and started scrubbing. I cursed the phantom shitter, I cursed the rough surfaces and the threadbare carpet, and I cursed my decision to ever become a pastor.

While I was swearing and cleaning, I could hear on the other side of the wall one of the AA groups that met at our church. As I scrubbed, I heard "The Serenity Prayer" seeping through the walls. I remembered the words on the back of that Michael's T-shirt Abby and I had made: *Stand up for Grace.* It's God's grace that inspires us and lifts us from the muck. The experience of cleaning was disgusting, but hearing "The Serenity Prayer," the reminder of God's grace, was a pretty good consolation prize.

■ ■ ■

Our little church in Greenpoint is run on a shoestring budget. So, between running a struggling church and cleaning crap off the basement floor, one of the ways we raise money, given our location, history, and the vintage look of the church, is offering it for movie shoots.

Believe it or not, we've had some famous visitors and have discovered this is an outstanding way to fund the ministry.

In the fall of 2009, we got a request for a movie shoot. It was to star Keanu Reeves and Vera Farmiga, and the good news was that they offered us a tidy rental fee for a short shoot. The bad news was that they wanted to shoot the movie over Thanksgiving week, which, since we started the hunger ministry, was one of the busiest weeks of the year. However, given Keanu's status as a lesbian sex symbol (trust me on this one) and the lure of cash that we sorely needed, I quickly agreed.

Thanksgiving week did not underdeliver. The phone rang off the hook with a combination of people needing food and wanting to donate to the hunger ministry. We had media inquiries and emails flooding our inbox. Queen Christine ruled with her iron fist, sans velvet glove. We were in the midst of a little game we call "Turkey Jenga," where we start with a few dozen turkeys and, throughout the day, have to deal with a combination of hungry residents who want them and kind-hearted donors who keep giving us more. Then, because we weren't busy enough, the production company called. Keanu and Vera wanted to do a walkthrough on the day of the Thanksgiving feast.

I was torn. Jen and our son, John, were already in Kansas City to visit her family. I stayed behind to orchestrate the Thanksgiving dinner, which now included Keanu Reeves. I have to admit, I was in full teenage crush mode—smitten by his stardom and excited that he would be shooting a movie in my church. I had already met him once, when he came with the location scout, and he was so unpretentious and sweet I knew we had already formed an indelible bond. In my mind, we were total bros.

The morning of the feast, I was excited and ready for Keanu and Vera. I was up early, dressed in my best pastor outfit, when the doorbell rang at eight a.m. I bounded down the stairs, ran to the front door and flung it open to greet them. Before me I saw Keanu Reeves, Vera Farmiga, and . . . a gigantic pile of human poop on the front stoop of my church. I froze. What does one do in this situation? Does one acknowledge the shit? Does one act like one doesn't see it? Luckily, my training kicked in. One of our congregants was a stage actor, and he taught me that if something out of the ordinary happens in a production (or, say, Sunday worship), the best thing to do was to acknowledge it and move on. That way, the audience isn't wondering whether the actor knows it's happening. You were doing the audience a favor by acknowledging it.

I decided this would be an outstanding opportunity to utilize that lesson; I should acknowledge the shit and move on. I sheepishly said, "I'm so sorry you were greeted with a pile of poop. We operate a soup kitchen that feeds many people who are homeless, and they sometimes don't have a place to poop, so they poop where they can. Today, I guess that place was in front of the church."

God bless Keanu. He acted like it was no big deal, saying, "Don't worry. Happens to everyone."

I thought, *No, Keanu, it does not happen to everyone. Tell me when this has ever happened to you! You are a wealthy, famous, lesbian-sex-symbol-actor, and I bet you have never awakened to find poop on your fancy stoop in Manhattan or Los Angeles or Hawaii or wherever you live.* But I kept my mouth shut and decided not to call him out on his ridiculous comment.

(By the way, for those who are wondering, I did eventually learn why poop was constantly showing up outside our front door. That portion of the front yard was surrounded by an iron railing that was a perfect tush-resting spot. Those who needed a comfortable place to relieve themselves found their stations atop that railing.)

During the shoot, they were in the church for rehearsals. After the shoot was over, Keanu had some trash from lunch and asked me where to throw it. I was just about to take out the kitchen trash, so I held out the trash bag, indicating that he should toss his in. He carefully placed his trash in the garbage bag and then took it out of my hands and walked it out to the curb. Yes, that's right.

Keanu Reeves takes out his own trash. Not just his own trash, but other people's trash as well! If he wasn't a sex symbol before, this sealed the deal.

You may be wondering which movie this was and how you can see it. I don't know if you can still find it anywhere. Although Keanu and Vera have sold billions of dollars worth of movie tickets, according to Wikipedia this movie grossed $102,000 in its domestic release. After that, I think it skipped cable, it skipped inflight movies, it skipped iTunes, and it was released directly on the Nintendo 64. This itself was a blessing. We got Keanu's rental fee and avoided the embarrassing discussions around the fact that, in addition to using the social hall and sanctuary for holding and catering, the movie also featured a sex scene shot in the parsonage. The movie's relative lack of success did not stop a very zealously devout Christian woman in Australia from emailing me relentlessly about how terrible it was that I had allowed the church to be used to film a scene that would encourage young girls to partake in premarital sex. I can't imagine that there were many ticket purchases by the aforementioned young girls in that whopping $102,000 box office take, but frankly, after meeting and talking to Keanu, I kinda saw where she was coming from.

Being human is a gift because it means no one is perfect. We are going to make mistakes and fall short. But we strivers have a hard time accepting our humanity—

we're committed to justice, impatiently. We can easily see the world as it should be, and not the way that it actually is. And I *really* have a hard time accepting that institutions, beloved institutions like the church or the fire service, are made up of humans. We make mistakes. As a result, our institutions make mistakes. And so, I can easily live in a state of non-acceptance. I can be a "detective of sin" rather than a "detective of grace." Acceptance is taking the world as it is, not as I would have it be.

To be clear, I am perfectly willing to acknowledge that not everyone will feel comfortable accepting Holy Shit as such an important element of this value. But stage wisdom helped me live out this value: once you acknowledge the muck itself, you can wait for God's light to shine through and see it for what it is—a sign of our humanity, even our frailty. Combine this with the Alcoholics Anonymous wisdom found in "The Serenity Prayer" and well, to me, it makes sense.

Most people know this part of the prayer:

> *God, grant me the serenity to accept the things I*
> *   cannot change,*
> *Courage to change the things I can,*
> *And wisdom to know the difference.*

But very few people know the entire prayer written by Reinhold Niebuhr.

Accepting hardship as a pathway to peace,
Taking, as Jesus did,
This sinful world as it is,
Not as I would have it,
Trusting that Jesus will make all things right,
If I surrender to His will . . .

Holding on to the anchor value of acceptance means not just knowing, but *expecting*, that there is going to be muck in my life at every turn. It means not wasting my time wishing it didn't exist, because it does. And it involves trusting that God's light will shine through it. I don't have to worry about trying to be perfect, or about holding anyone else up to a perfect standard. That's a lifelong lesson for strivers. And when all else fails (and it sometimes will, and I will sometimes be the cause of it), we can always *stand up for grace.*

7

WHEN YOU'RE IN A HOLE, STOP DIGGING

Integrity

I like to think of workability as a way to talk about integrity. If you think about a structure that collapses, engineers would say that it lacked structural integrity. It might have worked for a while, but at some point the lack of integrity caused it to become unworkable. Most of the time we have a good sense about the things in our lives that are actually working, and also about the things that aren't. Sometimes we like to avoid looking at the things that aren't working so well, and that's understandable. In our church we have closet that's in such disarray it's better to just keep the door shut. I used to think only our church had this problem. Space is at a premium in our small building, and every so often I'd get so frustrated I'd clean it out. Sure enough, a few weeks would go by and the chaos would creep back in. At one point, I got really exasperated and exclaimed, "Why can't people just put things back where they go?" One of our volunteers, who is Jewish, said, "We have a similar closet at my synagogue. It's a universal struggle."

The world as it is—with our church's disorganized closet, is obviously messy. It's not all bad, but it isn't as useful as we wish it were. And when a bin is packed with too much stuff, shoved into a spot where it doesn't really fit, and then keeps falling on someone—well, it's not exactly workable.

When something in my life breaks down, I try to reflect on where it was weakened. Usually I discover in one way or another, either implicitly or explicitly, that I gave my word to something and then didn't manage to keep it. If I promise to meet someone for lunch at noon but don't show up until 12:30, it doesn't make for a very workable get-together—especially if the other person only has a 45-minute lunch break. We give our word to some really important things, such as when couples make promises to one another in their wedding vows, medical professionals take the Hippocratic Oath, ministers say our ordination vows. And we give our word to seemingly small things when we say, "Sure! I'll meet you for lunch." Or, "I can volunteer for that task."

Sometimes when we give our word to things, we don't even know we are doing it. When we get behind the wheel of a car, there is an implicit expectation and agreement to stop at red lights and go when the light is green. (Don't worry, if you forget to go when the light changes to green in Brooklyn, you can be sure that the car behind you will honk to remind you.)

Living with integrity makes life workable. It isn't always easy, because life is messy ("holy shit" isn't a value for nothing). Being human is messy. I mess up a lot. Early on in life, my goal was to avoid the sting of making mistakes, so I tended to give my word to small things or maybe not give my word at all. I can easily be okay with missing one hundred percent of the shots I don't take rather than taking one shot and screwing it up. I don't like to screw up, and even more, I don't like the feeling I get in the pit of my stomach when I screw up, especially if I've hurt someone or I look foolish doing it.

It's still a growing edge for me to be open to making mistakes, or what I like to think of as *learning in front of others*. I'm not talking about realizing that, if I want others to put things back where they belong in the church closet, it would help to clearly label the bins and shelves so people have a guide for returning things. I'm talking about learning from others about my deeper, more painful areas that aren't working so well.

When I'm anxious, I tend to talk a lot without thinking. This often leads to problems. Some people talk themselves out of problems. I tend to talk myself into them. My father used to say, "When you're in a hole, stop digging." Sometimes he'd add, "You got yourself into a mess, now don't keep digging your way into a bigger mess."

I've gotten myself into plenty of holes. It took me a long time to trust that I might actually find a way out if I could just stop digging. Some of my extremely cringeworthy hole diggings that still make me feel ashamed have involved causing deep breaches in relationships. I have accidentally outed a gay clergy colleague, have used an offensive word I didn't realize was offensive, and have lost track of time and forgot to pick up my daughter on her first day of kindergarten. If you'd asked me if I believed it was possible to clean up those messes, I probably would have said, "No way." But living with integrity doesn't mean avoiding the mistake, acting like it didn't happen. For me, it's being brave enough to look at the mess and not just thinly apologize for it, but step into it—ask the people involved how my behavior impacted them.

The first time I consciously tried this, I thought the world was going to implode around me. I knew I had to clean up the mess. I knew I couldn't just run up to this person, hit them with the words "I'm sorry," and then run away. So I genuinely acknowledged my mistake, then asked, "Can you tell me how this impacted you?"

As the words left my mouth, my heart felt like it might start beating outside of my chest. I listened for the impact. It didn't feel good to hear it, but I kept breathing. I offered another sincere apology. And I committed to learning from my mistake and ensuring I did not do it again. Instead of my world, or that relationship, coming to an end, it actually became stronger, more fortified.

■ ■ ■

For a long time, I didn't want to acknowledge that I was avoiding the Hunger Program. Something wasn't workable about it, but it seemed overwhelming to examine the program at a deeper level. I had given my word to lead it but knew I wasn't really leading. When there was, finally, a real breakdown in its workability, again I thought the world would implode. It wasn't like I intentionally said, "Hey! I'm overwhelmed and don't know how to develop the systems and structures we all desperately need in order to work together." I didn't know what I didn't know. But once I started asking the volunteers what wasn't working for them, I saw that my passive leadership style, my desire to avoid conflict, harmed the program and harmed the people around me.

What came from that was a reorganization process that helped the Hunger Program become much more workable. And sure enough, just as we thought we had turned the corner, we'd discover other areas that needed attention. That's the joy of being fully human and fully alive—we are always going to find new mistakes, and new opportunities for learning.

Sometimes at the pantry a situation will arise that we couldn't have anticipated—or known how to plan for. Our existing manual for volunteers can guide us through a lot of tricky situations, and it's a good road-map for how we do what we do, but not every path is on the roadmap.

When the unanticipated happens, we've developed a really helpful sieve for sorting through how to respond. We ask the question, "Is it fair?" And if the answer to that first question seems to be "Yes," we follow it up with another question: "Is it fair to *everyone*?" Over the years, we've discovered that when we ask these two questions in a given situation, most of the time we end up with an answer on how to proceed.

■ ■ ■

In the summer of 2014, the police shooting of Michael Brown, Jr. in Ferguson, Missouri, gave rise to protests around police brutality, more widely illuminating the Black Lives Matter movement that began as a hashtag after Trayvon Martin was murdered. I'd like to think that our church was at the forefront of working for racial justice, but that isn't true. As a predominantly white church in a very white neighborhood, we weren't exactly a bastion of anti-racist action. It wasn't that we avoided talking about racism or weren't participating in anti-racism training. But it was clear the issue of racial injustice wasn't at the forefront of our work in the church or in the neighborhood.

That summer, the national conversation that emerged around Ferguson helped hold a mirror to our own faces. When Eric Garner was killed in Staten Island, the issue hit even closer to home. Our church community began talking about unequal policing and the criminal justice system in our city and state. Several members had relatives in prison or had been in prison themselves. The white members of our congregation knew how we experienced the police in the area, and it didn't seem to be the same as in other neighborhoods in the city.

In the fall, we chose to install a *Black Lives Matter* banner on the fence in front of the church. I hunted around online to see if the United Church of Christ offered such banners for their congregations to use. Not seeing any, I referred to the UCC style guide and designed one myself, then asked some fellow UCC pastors if any of them wanted to piggyback off our printing run. Yes, it turns out, several did. Soon I had fifty orders just from churches in Connecticut and Massachusetts. I also realized I had gotten myself into an organizational mess.

I wasn't sure how to upload the design to the printer's website and felt overwhelmed trying to figure out how to request shipment of the banners to so many different places. I figured I should call the printing company in North Carolina. Though given that it was a state in the South, I wasn't entirely sure what kind of welcome I would get when the company saw the message on the banner. On the phone, I explained to the woman taking the order why it went from one to fifty banners. I took a breath and waited for her response, and was surprised when she replied, "Oh, if that's what the banner says, I would like to pay for them myself."

With her help, all of the churches received the banners in less than a week. We installed ours in front of the church, and within a few days, it was vandalized. Someone added a comma and the words "so support cops." We ordered a replacement banner. It was vandalized again, this time with an em dash and the same words: "so support cops." I suppose our vandal didn't have a consistent copy editor.

After some prayer, the pastors and board decided to write a letter to all our neighbors, explaining why we had hung the banner and invited people to talk with us about it. Sure enough, the following week, a woman came in to speak with me about the banner. She was angry. She claimed that our banner would destroy morale among police officers, who needed our support in order to keep our neighborhood safe. I wanted to write her off, and I really didn't want to have someone yelling at me. My first instinct was to explain that the banner wasn't anti-police at all. I started to justify the banner. But I realized that if we invited people to come for conversation, then I needed to actually converse, or in this case, listen.

In situations of deep conflict, emotions tend to run hot. I've learned that I don't do my best listening when I'm amped up. Our church wanted to foster a conversation—because that's where we believed we might be able to talk about white privilege and the impact of racism. I realized that if I got quiet and listened to her, there was a better chance she might get quiet and listen to me.

It's easier for me to be open to hear someone who disagrees with me than it is to be open to someone who holds a mirror to my own integrity gaps. The moments when someone helps me see something I'd rather avoid are challenging. More than anything, I would love to say I'm not inclined to racial bias, but that's not true. I live in a society where racial bias is as prevalent as the air I breathe. It's the environment in which I've always lived. I benefit from being white in ways I don't even know about. And, even when I try my absolute best to be actively anti-racist, I can still operate out of my own internalized racist bias.

When I was a kid in Sunday school, around the time of our confirmation, the teacher gave us the opportunity to give our word to something big: a pledge that if we ever heard someone saying something racist we'd speak up about it. Maybe my longstanding fear of giving my word started there because I thought, *I am going to absolutely mess up on this.* It's not just witnessing racism in others and calling it out, but also calling out racism within our own selves. Sometimes I wonder what I actually learned in Sunday school. But I definitely remember the day we had the opportunity to say "yes" to this promise.

What I hadn't realized is that saying "yes" would mean committing not only to speaking out when others said or did something racist but also to correcting myself. I'm convinced it's one of the most courageous acts of love for someone to say to me, "Hey, I noticed you did this or said this, and I'd like you to consider how that sounded or felt to me." Recently, someone said that to me—and I rolled out a mix of justifying my actions, explaining myself, and then excusing what I had said. My emotions were in high gear—I felt uncomfortable, ashamed, embarrassed—and I wanted to do anything to get away from those feelings, and from the loving, brave person who said those words to me. Justifying, though, doesn't restore workability. In that situation, for our relationship to work in a healthy, loving way, I needed to see what I didn't want to see and hear the words I didn't want to hear.

I wish there were a simple process for anti-racist community building—for improved workability and deeper integrity. There isn't. It's hard work, and it is never done. The sin of racism impacts all of us. And the work of antiracism is all of our work. White people like me have to get far more comfortable with being uncomfortable if we care about making our communities safe and loving for everyone.

There's a late-night reality show called *Hardcore Heroes* (I encourage you to say that in your most macho-monster-truck-announcer voice: "Haaaardcooooore Heeeerooooes"). One episode featured Battalion Chief Jack Pritchard, a highly decorated firefighter, who described a particularly dangerous fire situation involving a baby trapped inside the back room of an apartment. He crawled toward the room, and when the heat got so high he thought about retreating, he told himself to keep going and count to ten. When he got to ten, he did it again—kept going and counting to ten. Eventually, he made it all the way to the baby and pulled the crib out.

The rescue got a lot of press, and Jack later received the department's highest award for his bravery. His model of pushing through discomfort—count to ten and keep repeating until you get through it—is something I've held on to when I feel overwhelmed. Especially in those moments where I thought facing the truth, whatever the truth might be, would do me in.

A few years after seeing this episode, I met Jack. I bounded up to him and introduced myself, saying, "Hey, Jack Pritchard! I'm Ann Kansfield, the chaplain. I saw your episode of *Hardcore Heroes* [I refrained from using the monster truck announcer voice]—and you taught me a really important technique." I continued, "You might not have intended it this way, but you taught me how to be uncomfortable." Jack's face lit up hearing that. "Yeah! Just keep counting to ten and keep on going."

Living a life of integrity is hard work. If you are a hole-digger like me, it's often uncomfortable work, especially when it matters the most. Do I mind if you tell me the closet at church is stuffed with things in the wrong spot? Sure. It's annoying. But the emotional stakes aren't too high. When my wife tells me that she doesn't want to go to another social event because I talk too much and she can't get a word in edgewise, well—that doesn't feel so good. We'd been married for over fifteen years when she bluntly told me one day, "Look, Ann, we just have different social needs. You're such an extrovert, you can't help yourself. We meet someone and you just talk and talk, and I can't get a word in edgewise. I'm tired of you crowding me out. You go to that party and I'll stay home."

She bravely told me the hard truth. I'm sure she had attempted to tell me some version of it before, but I wasn't able to hear it. I knew I had dug that hole. I also knew it was time to stop digging. She was right—and it hit a nerve. Deep inside, I probably knew I talked too much. But before I stopped digging, I tried to deny it. "Come on, that's not true. I let you talk as much as I do." She gave me a look that said, "That's a bald-face lie." So I picked up the next shovel: I justified myself *and* blamed her. "But you have to just jump in and talk!" As much I wanted to start conversations in our neighborhood, and as much as I knew that conversation is about *listening*, I really didn't want to hear what she was saying. I also wanted her to accompany me to a party that night. With my extraordinary hole-digging abilities, you might imagine it took me a while to receive her feedback as a gift. It also took me a while to hear that there might be times when she doesn't want to socialize as much as I do. Honestly, I can't understand why anyone might not like socializing as much as I do. I could socialize every day of the week and twice on the weekend. Accepting this required both the "stop digging" value *and* counting to ten.

Finally, we came up with a plan when it came to various social events. We developed a five-point scale: one was a totally optional, "I don't care if you come or not," kind of event, and five was a "I really want you, dare I say need you, to come with me and it's not really an option" kind of event. This way we could let each other know how important any given social event was for either of us. It became a helpful shorthand. I could say, "Hey! Want to come with me to the Mayor's Interfaith Breakfast? It's higher for me, but probably only a one on the need-you scale, so it's okay if you'd rather skip the mini bagels and salmon on tiny toast."

The other stop-digging practice that helped build better workability into our social life was for me to admit that I did, in fact, get so excited at social events that I'd forget Jen wanted to participate in the conversation. I finally threw down the shovel and asked for her help with this. We agreed that before we went out, she would gently remind me of this habit. Then I was to literally sit on my hands as a reminder to let others talk. Embarrassing to admit, but if you see me sitting on my hands at a social gathering, you'll know I'm so excited I have to physically restrain myself in order to shut up and listen.

8

SHOWING UP IS 99% OF THE JOB

Presence

Pastoring a small church in a neighborhood like Greenpoint proves over and over the old saying: *Ninety-nine percent of the job is showing up.* Usually, the situations I most want to avoid are the ones where I most need to show up. Moments of deep grief. Trauma. When I don't know what to say because there really isn't anything *to* say. Sometimes, all we can do is to be present with people—an authentic kind of presence, not preachy or forced.

Sometimes it takes people like Wilfredo to help us show up to ourselves and others. Wilfredo grew up on the north side of Greenpoint, back when it was predominantly Puerto Rican and known for having extremely high rates of alcoholism and domestic violence. I'm not completely unconvinced that the church didn't perpetuate that in some ways. It was part of the culture: people smacked each other around routinely or got drunk and wrapped their cars around telephone poles, and the attitude in the neighborhood and in its silent churches was that there wasn't anything anyone could do about it.

Wilfredo was one of ten kids in his family. I'm sure his parents didn't have it easy; they, like many others in the neighborhood, were pretty rough around the edges. Wilfredo bore the brunt of his father's anger and from an early age started acting out, getting sent off to a juvie residence by the time he was ten years old. He probably started drinking and drugging around the same time as his first run-in with the criminal justice system. He ended up hanging out at the Episcopal church in Green-point at that young age as well, and he spoke highly of the priest there who listened to him and cared about him. Wilfredo's positive experience with church at a formative age explains why, whenever he went through a rough spot in life, he ended up around a church.

I first met him when he was a few days sober, before an AA meeting at the church. The meeting wasn't super-functional with healthy boundaries: they gave him a key to the building and asked him to set up for the meeting. Not a good move, given he was only a few days sober. I walked into the church and saw a guy feverishly mop-ping the floor with a fanatical zeal to make it shine. (Or perhaps it was a better decision than I had realized?) We talked and he mentioned recently getting out of jail. I doubt anyone had ever given him an IQ test, but in our short conversation I realized this guy would have come out in the ninety-ninth percentile. Wilfredo knew a lot about a lot. Like, arcane things about New York State—facts about Buffalo, or Syracuse, or Watertown. I asked how he knew such facts and the answer was invariably, "Oh, I spent some time in (fill in the blank) prison." He was about fifty years old when we met and fully committed to staying out of prison. No wonder; he had spent more of his life in the system than out of it.

We soon hired him as our first janitor/sexton. Together we would have endless adventures. He was scary strong—lifting boxes the rest of us couldn't even budge. The only "hard" skill he learned in prison was painting, and he loved doing it. He could paint a room swiftly and with gusto, applying so much strength and pressure to the roller it would invariably cause little, almost invisible, specks to splatter around the room. I love seeing those specks because I know they came from him.

Just before Hurricane Sandy hit, I asked if we could use the parsonage at the South Bushwick Reformed Church to house our part-time church administrator, Charles. Charles came to us as an Americorp member, a program that places volunteers for year-long terms of service helping non-profits. He helped us secure some funding from the city that required detailed paperwork Jen and I had long since abandoned. With that funding, we were able to hire him part-time to do admin work after his Americorps term ended. He needed a place to live, which was going to be difficult given his part-time salary and the cost of housing in New York.

Asking for access to this unused parsonage was my solution. In exchange for use, we would fix up the space. My ultimate goal was to make it an intentional Christian community for young people who were moving to the city (a dream that ultimately never happened).

Wilfredo and I went to work fixing up the parsonage, which was in considerable disrepair. The more we dug, the worse it got. (And in this instance, it required we keep digging.) The pipes had frozen so there were tons of leaks and water damage. There were structural issues. And years of neglect had made it an uninhabitable space. I was having lunch with a colleague one day and invited her to come check out the work on the parsonage. As we approached, we saw Wilfredo on a ladder, painting the awning over the front door. When she got out of the car, Wilfredo yelled, "Hey, I know you!" and then proceeded to tell her where her church was. Many years earlier, he had needed a place to live away from Greenpoint, his family, and the abuse culture. He found a room around the corner from her church. They had a lunchtime ministry and she would give him sandwiches. Not only did he remember facts, he never forgot a kindness.

My first thoughts were: A, this guy has an incredible mind, and B, church really matters to him. In his youth, Wilfredo had developed a hobby of raising homing pigeons. This wasn't out of the ordinary in Brooklyn, especially "back in the day." He'd tell me about various aspects of raising championship birds and how they'd compete. Whenever he was in trouble, Wilfredo was like a homing pigeon flying back to church. He would disappear for a while, then resurface, and then disappear again. While we couldn't let him keep his job when he kept disappearing, that didn't stop our friendship. He was always eager to help, and I was always eager to hang out with him and learn from him.

Wilfredo came to the rescue dozens of times. When the city ran tests on our church and found fifty-four violations, and we had to have all of the radiators sandblasted at a shop in New Jersey, Wilfredo and I removed every single radiator, rented a U-Haul, and with the help of a couple of his equally strong friends, loaded every radiator into the truck. When the front gate of the church had sunk to the point where it would no longer open, Wilfredo used a car jack to raise up the gate so we could fix the hinge. When I asked him how he got the idea, he told me he used to use car jacks to break into buildings with roll-up security doors. I was not sorry I asked. There was nobody better at getting past locks. When we were locked out of any place, Wilfredo always knew how to get in.

Wilfredo had an infinite basket of skills, but he didn't always know how the working world ran to be able to apply them. He didn't know about calling in sick. Or about the importance of being on time when you say you're going to show up. He made me realize that it wasn't just smarts needed to hold down a job, but the kind of cultural, social knowledge that some people got from watching their parents or other adults in the community around them.

But what Wilfredo had mastered, and what I learned from him, was the importance of being present for the people he loved.

When I think about the anchor value of presence, of showing up for people in my life no matter what, it's some of our own congregants that come to mind as beautiful illustrations of what that looks like. People who may not have fit the typical qualifications of what we think of as "successful" but who taught me volumes about being present.

One Greenpointer named Todd was introduced to me through Danielle, a congregant who had briefly dated him. Todd had gone to detox and then checked himself out of rehab, not wanting to drink anymore but not knowing what to do with himself. Jen and I had recently bought a fixer-upper next door to my parents' house in the Poconos. We came to the transaction with three percent down and lots of prayers. The house was Jen's idea. She said I needed a hobby, but she also had an ulterior motive. Three of my four grandparents had died before I had much of a chance to know them. I always regretted not spending more time with them. So, I put a high priority on making sure my own kids would get to know their grandparents. When we'd visit my folks, it was a tight squeeze, especially when my brother and his wife would also come to visit. We figured if we got the house nearby, it would give us a little room and help our kids get to know my parents.

After buying it, I set to work to make it useable. It needed a new kitchen, starting with the floor—the old one was rotted-out linoleum. While I was scheming about how to get a new floor, Todd got in touch with me, asking for some advice. He needed to get away to a place where it would be impossible for him to get his hands on booze, and he needed to stay busy. Perfect. I said, "Well, I can keep you company for the time being, but I'm about to go to the Poconos to put a new kitchen floor into my house. If you want to come and help me, I guarantee you will be unable to find any booze for miles because it's far too long a walk to get to the nearest convenience store."

Todd loved the idea, so we went and put in a floor. We enjoyed it so, much we put in a kitchen counter. We may have replaced the dishwasher that week as well. I don't know if he had ever put in a floor before; I certainly hadn't. There were moments when we weren't sure we had made a good choice by ripping out the old floor and ugly base cabinets, but in the end, it came together pretty well. And we had great conversations while we worked. Working on something together—whether it's cooking or serving a meal, organizing cans in the pantry, painting a wall, or putting in a new floor—is also a vehicle to connect and talk with one another. Maybe that's why quilting bees build community (although we haven't actually tried that yet).

I was on a learning curve about what it meant to show up, why it was so important to be present. And both Todd and Wilfredo were good unintentional teachers. I saw how showing up for others created community. As those lessons from Todd and Wilfredo deepened, I had an opportunity to be present for someone else, eighty-year-old Ada, who was struggling with her health and believed she was dying. Being present to her, with her, brought a sense of joy for both of us.

Ada was a beloved octogenarian who volunteered with the food pantry. She was a character. Picture an eighty-something woman who picks up her skirt at the food pantry to show everyone her Minnie Mouse panties. She would walk around the dinner crowd tossing out the free condoms that the city of New York sent to the church, saying, "Have some candy!" (The city clearly mistook our Reformed congregation for the Crystal Cathedral, because they gave us more condoms than our congregation could use in a hundred lifetimes.) Ada was a surprise and a delight to everyone who came to the pantry.

When she was no longer able to show up to the pantry, I was able to show up for her. I showed up when she was tired and weak. In her final weeks I sat with her and simply enjoyed her presence. One time, as I sat with her in the bedroom of her apartment, I heard her mutter something to her daughter in Spanish. From the kitchen her daughter yelled back, "No, Ma, she isn't gonna want a beer! It's eleven in the morning."

I turned to this beloved saint, and she whispered in her Puerto Rican accent, "Heyyy, Ana! This sick shit (long pause for emphasis), it fucking sucks." It's odd, maybe, but to me, her words sounded like a prayer. I'd known this woman for what felt like forever. She'd never called me Ann, only Ana. In just about every conversation, she tried to offer me beer, or more often, weed (always pronounced mari-ju-ana, and smoked out of a penis-shaped pipe that she wore as a necklace). She told me that when I'm in my own decline, my life will be better with those two things in it. But really, my life right then was just better with her in it.

Person after person. Life event after life event. Broken-down space after broken-down space, of illness or building disrepair, I was learning what showing up meant. I was also beginning to understand that being present includes keeping yourself open not only to people around you but to God. In every event. Every. Single. Day.

Anyone who has watched a police procedural on TV knows about the concept of someone getting their "one phone call," but there is a little-known codicil to the rule. If you become a permanent guest of the Department of Corrections, you get one five-minute phone call per day. And given that Tom's first call with me worked out so well for him, he called me. Every day.

Tom was a man who was a semi-regular guest of the Hunger Program. When Tom got picked up by the NYPD on an open warrant one day, they took his phone. For some reason, the last time he had come to dinner he had taken the church bulletin with him, and for some other reason, it was in his pocket when he got arrested. When it came time for him to make his one phone call, the only number he had was the church number. So, he called us. In his one phone call, he asked if I might google his dad's phone number for him. I did. I thought my interaction with Tom was over, at least until he came back to the Hunger Program. I was wrong.

I don't want to make it sound like the calls were unwelcomed. Tom was an interesting, thoughtful person. He used the five minutes well. I learned a lot from him. For instance, apparently the Department of Corrections is very particular about what color socks you can send to someone—totally new info to me. These are among the many things they don't teach you in seminary. Eventually, Tom finished his time in New York and got extradited to Connecticut, where the rules were different. He didn't get to call, but he would write. One of the pieces of mail I treasure was an Easter card he drew me with a ballpoint pen. It had a bunny behind some bars and the caption read: *Jail sucks.* If I remember correctly, inside it said, *but you gotta believe in resurrections.*

About a year later, someone rang the church doorbell. I answered and he said, "Hi! It's Tom! I'm on parole." I gave him a big hug and said I was happy to see him and to see he was out of prison. My next thought was, *This guy is on parole and he crossed state lines—not good.* Lying, Tom assured me he was not breaking parole. Then he confided that he'd been drinking and he couldn't stop. Thinking all of this through, I said, "Look, Tom, you just got out of prison. You're on parole. You're drunk. And you've left the state. This is a bad idea from top to bottom. You do not want to go back to prison again. You gotta get yourself back to Connecticut."

He waffled. I took him to lunch. He continued to waffle. "Look dude, it's the day before Christmas Eve. It's now or never. I'll drop you off in Connecticut. *You need to get out of New York City!*" Still, he waffled.

The next day it was sleeting rain. Miserable. The doorbell rang, and sure enough, there he was. He'd thought about it and he wanted to go back to Connecticut. And, he said, he wanted to go to detox. I figured that was a good plan (stop digging and show up, two helpful and related values). He could check in to detox and call his parole officer and explain that he'd slipped but was back on track. I googled to find the closest Connecticut hospital over the state line. It was Greenwich Hospital. We drove in the awful, sleety, miserable weather up to Greenwich while I kept looking at my watch and hoping I could get back in time for Christmas Eve worship.

Entering Greenwich, I realized I was a fish out of water. It's a very wealthy town, and not exactly my scene. Between my life as a Greenpoint minister and an FDNY chaplain, I had by now visited most of the hospitals in New York City, but Greenwich might as well be on Mars. We were greeted with large estates surrounded by verdant, carefully manicured lawns. The downtown had every luxury store you could imagine. The hospital itself was spotless, making me think the clergy gossip about Greenwich Hospital was true: that when a baby was born the parents were served a surf and turf dinner.

We sat in the waiting room, surrounded by the best and brightest of the one percent of the one percent. The lesbian minister and Tom, who had jumped parole and wanted to be admitted to detox. As luxurious as it was, it was still a long wait, giving me plenty of time to gaze into one the most beautiful fish tanks I'd ever seen, and the richest fish in the tri-state area, which were swimming calmly and watching us with equal interest. I decided, right on the spot, that if anything ever happens to me, I want to be rushed to Greenwich Hospital.

One of the things you have to know about detox is that the person entering needs to be drunk in order to get in. So, Tom was pretty liquored up and had begun talking with Nemo, the beautiful orange fish in the expensive tank. Everyone in the waiting room was looking at us, and I was like, "Yeah, I'm his pastor friend." I'm pretty sure they'd seen drunk people before, but my guess is it was probably the folks getting liquored up at the Yale reunion, or local teenagers. They were not ready for Tom the paroled convict.

Being present with Tom definitely involved some of my more creative problem solving. Even as I write this, I wonder if I'm going to get in trouble for admitting to driving a parole breaker across state lines, but I'm going to assume that the statute of limitations has run out and I'm safe. (Also, I changed Tom's name for a little extra insurance.) Truthfully, I don't relish spending time with drunks. But even drunk, driving Tom to Greenwich was an unexpected, sweet blessing. It was probably the best Christmas Eve I've ever had. It was a privilege to be his chosen prison correspondent. Jesus says a lot about not forgetting people in prison, and there's a sacred kind of connection there. We tend to think Jesus was all about doing something for those less fortunate, but my view is that so many of his teachings are really about keeping *us* spiritually grounded, present. Tom did far more for me than I ever did for him.

■ ■ ■

When the news came out about my being sworn in as an FDNY chaplain, an article about it surfaced on the Breitbart website with such mean-spirited comments it stung. Still feeling the pain of it, I happened to witness my son, John, saying something hurtful to his younger sister, Grace. The easy, reflexive reaction was to immediately snap at him, tell him to apologize, point out how he was wrong. Instead, I tried a new tack and said, "People who don't know me have said mean things about me online. It doesn't feel good." We then read some of the hateful comments together. It helped my son see his negative behavior in a new way and, hopefully, will stick with him a lot longer than the fire and brimstone approach that first came to mind. Jen will tell you that the jury is still out.

Presence is about having the mindfulness to avoid the knee-jerk reaction, to contemplate the bigger lesson of a life experience, and to look for chances to communicate the experience in a manner that's deeper and more meaningful than what our initial response would have been. As a pastor, parent, funeral clergy, hospice bedside sitter, and the driver for off-the-wagon individuals getting back to the Connecticut border, I am attempting to practice that presence of mind and presence for others. I am on a continual quest to live that kind of truth in my own life.

Recently, Jen and I went to hear the film director John Waters talk about his movies, drugs, the Divine, and about something called anal bleaching which just went way over my homonormative, vanilla head. Someone asked him about how he was taking on Trump in his art, and what he said surprised and challenged me. It spoke to me—about being a faith leader, about presence, and about living our truth. He said he wants his films to be timeless, that being specific about various injustices

happening right now would date a film almost immediately. But the themes that need to be touched on now
more than ever are timeless; they are essential for today.

For someone who thinks about the teachings of
Jesus and is fixated on the current situation in our
country, I don't know how to make sense of every single
awful, unjust thing our government is doing on a specific day. There are so many. Some people are called to
name them one by one, and others feel called to name
the themes, the values they represent or challenge. Still
others look to the teachings of Jesus to help us live
out our values, to help us show up and be present for
justice or faith, or to dig fewer holes, and less deep. That,
I recognized, was something that called to me. I wasn't
expecting John Waters to teach me about the gospels,
but the Lord can be found unexpectedly most anywhere.

■ ■ ■

By this point you've probably guessed that our church at
Greenpoint attracts a wide variety of people. Every week
I think about how to be present for them even as they're
being present for church, each in their own way. In my
mind, everyone there is as human as I am, and each of
us is being saved by grace—and that unifies this dispa-
rate group. We share a common ground as we appreciate
our differences, and at the same time, take solace in our

common strength. If you make the trek to Greenpoint on a Sunday morning, you've not only made a serious commitment to the G train, but also to being present to the reality of who you are, and to a shared hope for grace. Simply showing up—for the people in your life, for God—that's ninety-nine percent of what it means to be part of a community. I imagine Wilfredo, Ada, and Tom might tell you there's nothing like it.

THERE'S ALWAYS MORE

Generosity

In the spirit of full disclosure, let me start this chapter by acknowledging that I'm cheap. Totally frugal. I come from people who use the drive-thru so they don't have to leave a tip. But even with that upbringing, I've learned that being cheap doesn't do me, or the world, any good. In the Gospel of John, Jesus said, "I came that you should have life and have it abundantly." An abundant life is one of generosity—not just with our money but with our time, our presence, our love, our prayers. There are lots of ways that we can choose to be stingy or generous, but a lack of generosity is ultimately an affront to God.

The motto of the Greenpoint Hunger Program—"The vision of the day when sharing by all means scarcity for none"—paints a picture of generosity and community and speaks to each person's agency. It isn't about charity, it's about sharing. In Jewish tradition, the ultimate form of charity is when neither the giver nor the receiver knows each other. This creates a kind of humility on the giver's side and dignity on the receiver's side. It also helps the giver understand generosity isn't just for the recipient, it's something you do for yourself.

In one of the most watched episodes of the television show *ER*, the beloved Dr. Green lies on his death-bed, looks at his teenage daughter, and says, "Be generous." As a cheap tightwad learning to add generosity to my list of core anchor values, I constantly ask myself: *In what ways am I the beneficiary of my own generosity?* The answers are many. Sharing generously brightens my day. Giving things away, particularly things I want for myself, has an inverse effect—I'm not lessened by giving, I'm filled. It helps me connect with others. It reminds me that when I die, I'm not taking anything with me, so I might as well share it with the people I meet. And true generosity, I'm learning, is moving beyond just material resources. To use the old church line, at its best it encompasses time, talents, and treasure.

The miracle of the feeding of the five thousand as recorded in the Gospel of Matthew was a miracle of distribution, not multiplication. How did it happen? Perhaps the people who were gathered there saw a kid take out his loaves and fish and, witnessing his generosity, were inspired to share what they had as well. In an earlier chapter, I mentioned that every Thanksgiving we play Turkey Jenga and I become a turkey broker of the local neighborhood fowl market. One year all of Greenpoint got involved and it was the best game ever.

Here's how it works: each year a business in Greenpoint donates a bunch of turkeys to us in honor of the local police precinct. The cops call, ask us how many birds we need, usually insist that we need more, then the business schedules a drop off. One year it was thirty turkeys. The day before Thanksgiving, they dropped off eighty turkeys. I figured they upped our number, no big deal. I had just gotten a call from a colleague who needed more turkeys for their community meal, so I said, "Come by and get them; we have extra this year!" I gave him forty of the extra fifty and the other ten went to an organization that works with immigrants. The colleague thanked me profusely when he picked them up, saying we were saving him as he had ordered a bunch of turkeys that had somehow gone missing.

After he left, I got a call from the turkey delivery guy saying they'd made a horrible mistake and dropped off too many birds. I freaked out because those extra birds were already given away to folks who needed them. The delivery guy freaked out because he was down fifty birds. When I asked him which organization was supposed to receive the missing turkeys, he said—yes, you guessed it—my colleague's church. Sharing is a generosity that works in so many dimensions. And Turkey Jenga, for me, is a way of *sharing by all means, scarcity for none.*

Generosity inspires generosity. That's where the multiplication comes in. Over the years with the Hunger Program, I have seen our generosity engender generosity in unexpected ways. One involved a guest named Bobby, who was one of my least favorite guests. He had a serious drug problem and was an irritant at the Hunger Program. He always had a negative comment and was always breaking the rules. I would assume it was his addiction acting out, but still, I did not enjoy spending time with him. Until one Thanksgiving, when Bobby came and thanked me for always feeding him. He then announced that the previous week he had spent all his money on booze and drugs, but this week he might as well share what he had by donating to the dinner. He pulled out $10 and handed it to me. This guy who was a perpetual thorn in my side gave me $10 to help feed others. Never in a billion years would I have imagined him handing me his drug money and asking me to spend it on dinner for everyone. But as someone who had experienced generosity on a regular basis, Bobby felt the need to practice it himself.

After we started the Hunger Program, one of the early large donations came from a neighbor who worked as a census taker. She had lost her corporate consulting job during the recession, so she figured she'd make ends meet by knocking on neighbors' doors doing the census. Before she'd lost her job, she had a very comfortable middle-class life in Greenpoint. However, the experience opened her eyes to the depth of poverty in our neighborhood. She eventually got a new job, and when she got her first paycheck, she donated her entire census earnings to the program.

When I first came to work as a chaplain for the New York Fire Department, one of the stories I heard involved Father Mychal Judge, an FDNY chaplain who died on 9/11. He'd walk around NYC with a pocket full of dollar bills, giving them to people asking for money on the street or in the subway. That story reminded me of a seminal article Pope Francis had written on generosity. He said it was not enough to throw a few coins at the poor; we needed to look them in the eye, greet them. We needed to acknowledge their humanity and their basic need to be connected with society. He said it was best to have a blanket rule that said whenever anyone asks, give each person one dollar so that you avoid needing to make a decision each time, and thus free yourself from the implicit evaluation of need. (By contrast, one of Francis's own American bishops, a few months later, urged his flock *not* to donate because it encourages a few dishonest professional panhandlers and sustains an unhealthy degrading lifestyle.)

On September 11, during the first year of my chaplaincy, inspired by both Father Judge and Pope Francis, I set out with a bunch of dollar bills in my wallet to give away. I offered people money, but what came back to me was so much more. In giving people my time and my presence, by stopping and sharing and truly engaging others as fellow children of God, I received the greater gifts. For anyone having a crappy day, I would say get out and give away money to people who ask. Don't worry about what they spend it on. Once you give a gift freely, it's out of your hands.

As for that bishop's views on giving? Here's one of the things I've learned running the Hunger Program: whenever people accuse others of some sort of bad behavior, they often have a similar one hidden in their back pocket. I used to think that was a myth, but Wall Street taught me to follow the numbers. It's turned out to be true every single time. Refuse to give on the grounds of someone sustaining a degrading or dishonest lifestyle? Take a look in the mirror. The secret will come out sooner or later.

Don't get me wrong, not all of my experiences with donations to the Hunger Program have been universally positive. Pastoring a church and running a hunger program have helped me see the good side and bad side of donations. How can there be a *bad* donation, you might wonder. Let's just say that people love to drop any kind of shit on a church—and I mean that literally and figuratively. I came up with a line just to let people know where I stand on this: *If you don't want it in your house, don't bring it to God's house.* A little excerpt from my perpetually unfinished second book, tentatively titled *Dispatches from the Hipster Vortex*, illustrates my point.

The church phone rings, waking me up at eleven thirty-five p.m. I remind myself that I do not need to answer every call at every hour, and let it go to voice-mail. The phone rings again. Fearing it's the dreaded middle-of-the-night-pastoral-care emergency, I answer.

A young, happy, white-guy voice chirps: "Hi! You have a food pantry, right?"

Me, tired and lethargic: "Ahhh, yeah."

YHWGV: "K. We're just having a party down the road and we ordered way too much food. Can we, like, give it to you tonight?"

Me: "Ahhh, what?"

YHWGV: "Caribbean food. We ordered too much. We were just gonna throw it out, but can't you use it?"

Me: "It's almost midnight. How about we talk about it tomorrow when I'm awake?"

YHWGV: "Yeah, well. We can just drop it off tonight."

All I can think about right now is getting his number so that when my kids wake me up at six a.m. tomorrow and ask to play with my phone, I can tell them to call him.

The Hunger Program does add a few stress points. Some force-give leftovers. Others take stuff from the church without permission. I mentioned Sara Miles and her food program before. I recall something in one of her books, a response she gives to a question about people taking extra at the food pantry. She says, "It isn't stealing if we were going to give it to them anyway." Most of the time, I'm capable of that generosity of spirit. But sometimes we *really* need the tools for ministry that we have, and we lose things we do *not* intend to give away. For example, someone took the metal ramp used for getting cases of food up the steps and into the sanctuary. Another time, someone took a big bag of potato chips Jen had bought for the Sunday potluck—I know, who doesn't like Ruffles? The final straw was the time when someone cracked open some tuna and crackers snack packs, and *only ate the crackers!* Every time something like this happened, it left us scrambling. Just because we were going to give it away doesn't mean we were going to give it to you, and by taking the entire bag, you kept others from enjoying it. This is the "Tragedy of the Commons," and it's played out in many soup kitchens.

Give time, talents, and treasure. How do I know when it's November? The church phone rings off the hook with people inquiring about volunteering at the soup kitchen. No one wants to hear that we get too many volunteers for Thanksgiving and the *actual need* is for people who will volunteer regularly throughout the year. These are the lessons I'm learning as I lean into this anchor value of generosity. Sometimes it gets messy and complicated. As in all of life, grace needs to be applied in heavy doses as I learn to do life with the community around me and attempt to give freely of my time, money, and especially myself.

■ ■ ■

My role with the fire department has given me a different window into sharing, with unexpected opportunities to see generosity at work. Recently, I was called to a three-alarm fire in the Bronx. I'd already had a full day and the last thing I needed that night was a call way out to the Bronx. It was raining and cold and dark—pretty miserable. I did not want to go out, but I took off the jammies and put on the thermals.

When we got through traffic and made it to the fire, I checked in with the chief and walked around to Emergency Medical Services to see if anyone was injured. No injuries, but there were lots of very cold, displaced residents, and it was thought that one of the buildings might have been a shelter. Some people say, "Fire doesn't discriminate," but it sure seems to happen often in lower-income residences. It's a sadness on top of a sadness. As is usual for big fires, the Red Cross takes some time to arrive. In the meantime, people are cold and wet and don't know if they have a place to go home to or not. They have questions for which there often aren't any answers, at least not for hours and hours. And while my primary job is to attend to the needs of the firefighters, I sometimes provide care for displaced people, especially if it helps the FD and related EMS focus on what they need to do.

This night several of our EMS members were concerned about the cold, wet, displaced residents. Someone was in the process of getting a city bus for them, and I volunteered to go over to White Castle to buy them some food. They could stay inside, eat, and get warm. I walked over and saw one or two firefighters there, along with a family of five. I asked the family if they'd eaten, and it was clear they had not. I asked the kids what they wanted, then I ordered fifty sliders and a bunch of drinks. I realized it was more than the family would eat, but I worried I wouldn't have enough for everyone outside. I didn't have a ton of money, but I had enough. I told myself we'd start with this and if we needed more, I could come back and get it.

I wanted to get back to my rounds outside, so I leaned over to two of the kids who were probably about five or six years old and said, "I ordered a bunch of sliders and here's a stack of cups for drinks. You're in charge now. Can you make sure that everyone who comes in here shares the food?" The kids gave me a huge smile and started joyfully going around handing out cups. I went back to the fire, checked in on some others. A half hour later the city bus arrived, and the displaced people got in and sat down. A guy who I would bet was the manager of White Castle walked over and said, "Anyone who needs coffee to warm up, come on inside. It's on me." Something was up. I had asked this manager earlier to give me a discount. He eventually agreed, but it wasn't a very big one. Now, here he was, giving out free coffee at eleven p.m. in the Bronx. That had to be a sure sign of the apocalypse or something.

Somebody came and told me they wanted to see me inside the White Castle. The place was completely packed. I figured they were running low on food. Or heck, maybe there was a food riot going on, with people fighting about who ate what, or who was getting more food. People get desperate in situations like this. But neither hypothesis was true. People just wanted to say thank you. The kids had given out sliders and drinks and everyone seemed happy. I couldn't believe it when I opened the box of sliders—it was like the miracle of the feeding of the five thousand. The White Castle was jammed to the rafters, and somehow there were still sliders left over!

Again, the miracle wasn't about multiplication, I realized. Here, it was about generosity. I looked over to see one of the firefighters buying someone a drink and cheese fries. Some EMTs came in to warm up, and I think they shared what they had as well. Before I left, I took a photo of the remaining sliders, in case I might not believe that this miracle had actually occurred. But when I got home, I thought of Doubting Thomas, well-known skeptic of the gospel story. Thomas wasn't a hero; he was a cautionary tale. To stay true to my God, I'm not going to print the photo out as proof, but I will bless all of you who believe me without seeing the burgers.

Being truly generous, I'm discovering, is a call for each of us to be present as a human being and a member of society. New Yorkers describe September 11 as the day they experienced hell on earth. But many New Yorkers will also tell you how, in the days and weeks after that awful day, we experienced incredible kindness, love, and generosity. Mixed with our grief was a taste of heaven on earth. We spoke to one another gently and talked to neighbors we previously wouldn't have known. People *offered* to let others go ahead of them in lines. Cars made way for others when merging. All the jerky, selfish behavior many of us usually practiced seemed to fall away. In retrospect, it felt like, for a short period of time, we all lived generously in the moment, not in the future or even in the past. We made time for one another.

In the years since 9/11, there have been many memorial events honoring the bravery, mourning the losses. One September 11th, I was driving from one event to another and I got stuck in traffic. I was already anxious, and as I tried to merge into a long line of cars waiting to go through the Holland Tunnel, no one was letting me in. I wanted to scream, "Hey! Why aren't you driving like it's that sacred time of 9/11! You just cut off the FDNY chaplain on her way to a memorial event, you jackass!"

That 9/11 spirit of love and compassion and generosity, well, we *all* miss it. It's difficult to remember to be generous with our love. It's even more difficult to be generous when others aren't as loving or kind as we want them to be. Today, take time to open your hearts up to people you don't know, and live in the moment. There's no rush. Today is the only today. Enjoy every minute. Share it. It will more than double. I've worked at numbers a long time. I observed the White Castle math—I know it's real.

DRESS UP YOUR HOLY SPIRIT GOGGLES

Perseverance

As the years passed and the church continued to grow toward health, there came a time when I looked back at when I had first arrived and thought, *Wow! Saying yes to this call was totally foolish. No wonder it was so hard for them to find a pastor—who would have wanted to come to a church with eight people?* That, I came to realize, was part of the miracle. At the time, I had no idea how big a job it would be. The congregation had no idea what they were agreeing to. And even though positive change feels good, the work of change was, and never is, easy.

On my first official Sunday at Greenpoint, as I mentioned, we had three congregants. After worship, we had a little family get-together with my cousins, all serious churchgoers. I told them all about how worship went and mentioned we had three people. My younger cousin Danny said, "You know, the Father, the Son and the Holy Spirit were there too. You gotta count them; that's three more right there." We laughed, and made the new count.

I've since come to refer to that time and sense of foolhardy adventure as my having worn "Holy Spirit Goggles"—like beer goggles, but with the Holy Spirit instead of booze. When you're willing to throw caution to the wind and take a leap of faith, you end up seeing the world through Holy Spirit Goggles. What once seemed impossible somehow became oddly reasonable. Still odd, but reasonable. Therapists refer to this as "reframing" a situation. Developing our ability to reframe life from one perspective to something closer to God's perspective changes things. While it's a metaphor of reframing, I still like to think of Holy Spirit Goggles as a value.

What things in life do we need to see differently? What would happen if we saw the world through God's lenses and not just our own? What if we did put on Holy Spirit Goggles? What would that change?

At Greenpoint we get plenty of opportunities to use Holy Spirit Goggles. You may say the church building is small and can cramp you, but that smallness was also the way that the church was able to stay open during the difficult years. It doesn't require much maintenance.

It's cheaper to heat and cool. And the mortgage is paid off, which frees us up to be grateful for the legacy of our ancestors. Reframing the Hunger Program work that we do as a participation of Jesus's miracle of the feeding of the five thousand—although without Jesus's full tool kit, we undertake distribution rather than multiplication—is an ongoing opportunity to wear Holy Spirit Goggles.

I also see constant opportunities to reframe my own life's journey. The financial downturn and loss of my job provided me with an amazing window to dive into the faith and service work I loved. Without that opening up, you would not be reading this book, and, in fact, I might be asking you to invest your 401k money with me. *That's* a miracle.

Once you experience the benefits of seeing with Holy Spirit Goggles, you realize that you can use them in almost every interaction. Jen and I were at a church conference where someone made an announcement over the PA system about a workshop related to youth ministry. The announcement said something ominous like ". . . only one third of young people in America are being raised in the church." Jen turned to me and said, "I don't know why they don't see that as good news. This way there will be fewer people infected with bad theology from an early age, and we won't have as much work to do to help them deal with the lifelong impacts of such bad theology in adulthood."

Many people lament the changes in Greenpoint related to a rezoning of many areas from industrial to residential back in 2005, which has, in part, led to rapid gentrification. Yes, it's true. The changes have been difficult for people who have had their rents raised and been forced to move. It is easy to lament what has been lost and to tilt into anxiety and fear for the future. I often forget to see through the goggles when I think about all of the people who have come to the church only to get married and/or have kids and then move away. We have a constant revolving door, not like the church in my neighborhood growing up. It's harder to see some of the possibilities that the future holds when there's so much change. But with the Holy Spirit Goggles, I become more capable of trusting in God's providence and seeing the future full of potential and hope.

The goggles come in handy in all sorts of life situations. A couple of years ago, I had to represent the church in court, which happened to be located just off Wall Street. Our wonderful pro bono lawyer came with me, and as we exited the building, Jim Cramer (from the TV show and podcast *Mad Money*) walked by. Since I was wearing my clerical collar, I stuck out my hand, introduced myself, told him about the Hunger Program, and asked him for a donation. He said yes. As he went on his way, a guy looking through a nearby trash can for food approached me and said, "I heard that you provide food to hungry people. I'm hungry. How can I get some food?" I explained where we were located, gave him my card, and assured him that if he could get out to Greenpoint he'd eat plenty of food. As this man went on his way, Jim Cramer returned, handed me a check and said, "Here you go. I didn't want you to think I was a bullshitter."

Our lawyer friend looked at me and said, "Now I get what you guys do. You're able to talk with a guy like Jim Cramer and ask him for money. He'd have most likely never given money to that homeless guy, or been able to get him food, but he'd write a check to you guys. You turn that money into food, and you're able to talk with that homeless guy and make sure he's fed. You're the middleman!" It was like Wall Street broker meets Holy Spirit Goggles.

I mentioned earlier that I'm short on grandparents, so I adopted one. Carol Hageman. Carol was the single biggest influence on the growth and development of our church. She and I would talk every day. Daily, I'd tell her some very small thing that was a move forward and she would affirm it, big time. I told her, "This church is a diamond in the rough. And so am I. Not many people believe either of us will amount to anything, but we know we are going to do big things together." I'll admit, that was some "Holy Spirit Goggles" perspective there.

When I started working with the church, I thought they were such a fabulous, wonderful, healthy church. I never thought, "Geez, there must be a reason there are only eight people in this church." I never saw it that way. Holy Spirit Goggles are the means by which we develop resilience, and resilience leads to perseverance. On a rare occasion, I might pause long enough to marvel that I could spend fifteen years attempting to turn a church around. But truly, this is a lifelong project, a "lifestyle choice" that has required a level of continued focus and commitment I never thought I had. I'm the person who took trombone lessons for a year, then switched to the flute, then gave up music altogether the following year to join the track team. Yet, I have been able to stick with this grand adventure all these years, always thinking, *Wow! This is amazing! We are right on the cusp of something totally exciting!* That's totally the work of Holy Spirit Goggles.

Sometimes, Holy Spirit Goggles alter the perspective of just one challenging day. This past year I spent a morning at an FDNY Memorial Day event, which included being present for several thousand firefighters as they marched past the families of firefighters who died this past year. Then I attended a luncheon where some chiefs and I dreamed up a fundraiser for the soup kitchen that involved a "Facial Hair of the FDNY" competition. I returned to the church to interact with our new bookkeeper. Then a sober guy who went out on a major bender came by because he knows I keep spare cigarettes to exchange for helping out around the church. There was a horrible stink in the basement—five giant rats the exterminator had sent to heaven when he'd set traps last week. I left to pick up my kids and said thanks to a retired RCA pastor who goes around fixing church buildings and who is strongly opposed to the ordination of LGBT ministers. He was up on a forty-foot ladder to fix our roof. The dude who tried to get my dad fired twelve years ago was fixing our roof. He needed the help of a carpenter, so I introduced him to Billy, one of our soup kitchen volunteers, who'd only had three beers so far today, so he got up on the roof to investigate what was going on. Now, the Rev. and Billy were both on my roof, and I wasn't sure either of them was qualified to be up in the air. I just prayed that the not-keen-on-me-being-ordained-Reverend and drunk (though far less than usual) Billy did not fall off the ladder. Now *that* would have been a real buzz kill.

That day? Proof that we need Holy Spirit Goggles.

Perseverance does not necessarily take a lot of skill. It just takes stubbornness. It takes not giving up. It requires keeping on keeping on. The trick is to not get dissuaded or freaked out or tricked into believing that your effort is futile. It helps block out external influences that might convince you to stop or give up. I find it helpful to look to the people who came before me— to the ancestors, as it were—and see how they persevered. To note how far they pushed forward and to imagine the struggle and courage it took to persevere through whatever difficulties they may have faced. We do not do this thing called *life* alone. In fact, there are countless people in community with us, the ones who have gone before us, blazing a trail, and the ones who cheer us along the way, helping us persevere in our own race.

11

PLEASE AND THANK YOU

Gratitude

You've met Christine, beloved friend and soup kitchen chef. She was honest about why she volunteered every Wednesday. She said she got far more out of it than she could ever give, and it helped her "put some gratitude in her attitude." When I'm discouraged, I still recall her voice (along with some kickass expletives) reminding me to do just that—put some gratitude in my attitude. Gratitude is one of those values that can't be separated from other values. It's integral to presence, necessary for a Holy Spirit Goggles perspective, the flip side of generosity. Each value builds on the others, complementing and enhancing them.

When one of us was in a foul mood, we'd often share our gratitude lists with each other. Christine once told me that when she couldn't think of anything to be thankful for, she'd toss her keys on the ground to force herself to her knees to look for them. When she found them, she would be grateful both for her keys and for her knees. Sure enough, every time we shared our gratitude lists, after about the third item, we'd turn our attitudes around.

I've written about the matriarchs in the congregation, especially when we were a small gathering, teaching me about prayer. They also taught me about faithfulness. About stubborn hope. These people allowed me to be myself. Lovingly supported me. Put up with my crazy ideas. Grace would often say something like, "Well, kid, we tried that one before but knock yourself out. Just don't ask me to do the work of it. I'm too old for that right now."

And we've been able to develop as a church without so many expectations. Maybe it's that G train line thing. We aren't so close to other churches that we compare and dissect our many failings. When we might be prone to that, we believe our context is different and we are unique, requiring a lot of ecclesiastical off-roading.

■ ■ ■

When I was named the first gay chaplain for the FDNY, the *New York Times* made a request to the fire department that they be able to break the story. The reason for this was that one of the editors for the *Times* was connected to the congregation. Luckily for both of us, the department agreed.

The editor assigned one of his brand-new reporters to write the story—Tatiana Schlossberg. In truth, I wasn't terribly excited about being interviewed. Tatiana had a deadline, and she caught me on a busy day. I told her if she was going to get her interview, she'd have to drive around with me on some errands: picking up kids from daycare, picking up paint for some renovation on the church, things like that. And given that we were driving around New York City on a very busy day, I might have used a little bit of profanity.

As we drove, we talked about our families, and, of course, about our religious backgrounds. Tatiana told me she was raised Catholic, and that, whenever her family was traveling, no matter what country they were in, her mother would find a Catholic church and try to attend daily Mass. Tatiana lamented that she had fallen away from church and expressed some interest in finding her way back. Although I would have been happy to take on that job myself, I am also friends with a renowned Jesuit theologian, Father Jim Martin, and offered to put her in touch with him.

The article ran. It was Tatiana's first profile piece as a *Times* reporter, and she did an amazing job. However, I realized that I might not have taken it as seriously as I should have. I was exhausted when Tatiana interviewed me. I shouldn't have been swearing, and I could have at least offered complete sentences instead of fits and starts while lane-dodging in traffic. I certainly never imagined it would run on the front of the Metro section. If you search it out on the *New York Times* website, you might notice that in the picture, I'm wearing pink sneakers, and you may ask yourself, *What kind of statement was Ann trying to make with the pink sneakers?* Sadly, the answer was (and still is) that I didn't pay attention to what I was wearing that day, and I am still mortified that I wore pink sneakers.

Anyhow, I didn't think much more about the piece beyond a mix of excitement and pink-shoe cringe. But about a week after it ran, someone asked how it felt to be interviewed by John F. Kennedy's granddaughter. *Who?* Tatiana (short pause) Schlossberg. The bell went off. Her mother? Yeah, that would be Caroline Kennedy Schlossberg. I thought, *Holy shit! How lucky am I?* Thank God I suggested she talk with Father Jim Martin about reconnecting with her Catholicism. I would have been mortified if I had tried to convert her to Protestantism; if it had worked, I would have been public enemy number one to every elderly Irish Catholic in the country!

Tatiana soon moved on to cover the morning news roundup. I'm pretty sure this involved staying up until three a.m. and condensing whatever was going on in New York City down to a single column. My sense is that it may have also involved spending several early morning hours alone. As a way to amuse herself, Tatiana decided to use her daily New York City news roundup as a way to have a little fun. In 2015, at the bottom of the roundup, she announced that the *Times* was going to be naming a "New Yorker of the Year." Her list of nominees included Lin-Manuel Miranda, The New York Mets, Pizza Rat, Donald Trump, and, in a surprise showing, *the Reverend Ann Kansfield.*

Holy Spirit Goggles being off at the moment, I knew that the only reason I was on the list was because Tatiana had done my write-up, and in a world where journalists are measured by their ability to generate clicks on the website, this was a good opportunity to pump her own content. (In case you haven't caught on by now, Tatiana is whip smart.) She announced that people should vote for their winner in the comments section of the article. Pink shoes aside, this was an opportunity. Come to find out, it was easy to create a profile and make comments in the *New York Times.* I went to my pastor's Facebook group and made my plea—even though it was the Fourth Week of Advent, a busy time for ministers. My people, and possibly more, came through for me.

I'm not going to read too much into the results. Lin Manuel and his dad clearly missed the paper that day, and his Google alert is probably so long he doesn't read it all the way to the end. The New York Mets haven't won a thing since 1986, so why start now? Pizza Rat's friends and family don't have opposable thumbs. And the outcome—me being named New Yorker of the Year—was a moment of pure gratitude. Gratitude for meeting Tatiana, gratitude for winning a silly award, and several years later, retroactive deep gratitude for solidly beating Donald Trump.

At my next FDNY event, the emcee played it up in a totally sweet way: "And the 2015 *New York Times* New Yorker of the Year is our own chaplain, the Reverend Ann Kansfield!" And you know what? Tatiana's little goof became a tradition. She moved on to greener journalistic pastures, but in 2016, a new writer took up the mantle, and in a stroke of genius for him (and luck for me), he asked me who I would nominate. Which then gave me the chance to lift other people and share the gift of friendship. Lifting up other people is its own form of gratitude. I loved nominating others and writing about the impact they've had on me.

When I was nominated and written up in that feature piece, I hadn't even thought about documenting my kick-ass values, but some of the things I said in the article reveal they were part of my DNA all along. When asked, "What makes a model New Yorker?" I said, "Someone who loves the city and all of the people in it. Somebody who is willing to interact with strangers, because what makes a New York moment is when strangers connect and suddenly it becomes a small town. (Someone with) creativity, compassion and the ability to really be authentic."

Through the nomination process I've been able to "pass it on" and recognize people both well qualified and very special to me, including Sergeant Hameen Armani, a Muslim-American NYPD officer who was instrumental in removing what looked like a terrorist bomb out of Times Square that year, and Ray Pheifer, a former firefighter who was suffering from cancer, the result of working at Ground Zero after 9/11. I was grateful for both of these brave civil servants and for the opportunity to lift them up in a public way. I was seeing how practicing the anchor value of gratitude could have a "pay it forward" effect.

■ ■ ■

Years ago, and planning far in advance, my wonderful wife used all of her executive functioning skills and bought us *Hamilton* tickets for an April 20, 2017, show. She knew Easter was that Sunday, so she figured by Thursday we would be rested, relaxed, and ready to enjoy this special treat. Sadly, that became a tragic date for the FDNY. On that same April day, a firefighter named

William Tolley died in the line of duty. All of the chaplains were called to the hospital, and as I left the apartment, I said to Jen, "Don't worry. I'm not going to miss our big date." *Hamilton* was a true sensation in the New York theater world. Tickets were almost impossible to get. I wanted Jen to know that I appreciated her and the effort she put into getting those tickets. I wasn't going to forget about it; I knew this was special. You might wonder, "How could anyone forget they have *Hamilton* tickets?" Well, my friends, I'm really great at being in the moment. So great that I can forget just about anything that isn't right in front of me, especially when being in the moment involves showing up for something that really matters.

During the day, I texted and called Jen to update her on the situation. I suggested that perhaps she walk over to the box office and see if they might exchange the tickets. Even so, I kept reminding her, "But if you can't exchange them, I'm not going to miss it. I'll be there." When my chaplain colleague learned we had these tickets, he said to me, "You tell Jen you're not going to miss that show. I'll see to it that you leave here with enough time to make it before the curtain opens." And he was right. I could have left. But Jen made the choice to give up the tickets, telling me, "Why be a chaplain for the fire department if you're not going to stay with your people in a time like this? This is the kind of moment that we have prepared for all along. This is what I gave you that blank check for when you signed on to the job. And plus, I have my wife right now, but someone else just lost their person today."

As this drama over the *Hamilton* tickets was going on in the background, the reality playing out in front of me felt far more important. Tragedy is gut wrenching and the raw emotional pain was everywhere. Everyone wanted to help, to be useful, to *do* something. My job was to pray, and you might think I had some experience with this, but in that moment, I felt out of my depth. How could my small Protestant prayers do the big job required of them? I didn't know what to do. I looked around, hoping another chaplain would show up so I could watch and learn from him. But traffic was bad and it would be at least a half hour before anyone else was able to get there. The fire commissioner must have seen my trepidation, because he paused long enough to give me a look of confidence and said something like, "You got this." And it was enough. Even when I wasn't sure I believed in my own abilities, and wasn't quite willing to trust in God, I was willing to believe that if the commissioner thought I could do it, I could at least act like it.

A group of us formed a circle around the beloved brother firefighter and I attempted to offer the best prayer I could. In my nervousness and insecurity, I totally forgot to say the Lord's Prayer. One of the guys from the union politely said, "Excuse me, Chaplain, but do you think we could say an Our Father?" I kicked myself for what I thought was a big fat error on my part. But you know what? I might have forgotten to say an Our Father, but *we* didn't forget it. Together we functioned as a team; we had one another's backs. During a period of intense stress, when I felt like I was letting down both my fellow firefighters and my wife, someone (or, more realistically, many someones) at least had mine, that's for sure. Clearly, it was for times like this that the word "gratitude" exists.

As the FDNY continued supporting the Tolley family, I continued my role as chaplain, and the opportunities for me to recognize gratitude as one of my anchor values continued. The FDNY is like a family. In a situation like this, incredibly painful and tragic, we all wanted to offer our very best to honor Firefighter Tolley. When the time came to attend the funeral, we dry-cleaned our uniforms and shined our shoes. We looked on point. It was something we could do. In the days following his death, I watched as various people attempted to offer words of solace and compassion. They showed up, offered gifts, hugs, tears—anything to try and make it better. Firefighter Tolley's funeral was a Catholic mass, so the non-Catholic FDNY chaplains sat next to two altar servers and eucharistic ministers on the side opposite the pulpit.

As for me, I sat next to two seasoned church ladies. I could tell they knew what they were doing and meant business as soon as I saw them. They radiated love, for their church and the people who comprised it, for their priests and for their ministries. Firefighter Tolley had left behind a wife and an eight-year-old daughter, Bella. As the priest gave the sermon, he shared stories about Billy and his family life, filling the sanctuary already rocked with pain and sadness with a fresh wave of sorrow. I learned that I'm a church lady in training when the two church ladies and I were the only ones singing along with the cantor the opening hymn, "Here I Am, Lord." We knew all the verses. And we didn't care that no one else was singing.

During the gospel acclamation, the musicians played a peppy "Alleluia" that I imagined might cause some of the older folks to roll their eyes. The church ladies, though, were downright *enthusiastic* about it, clapping on the beat. One of them looked toward Bella and the other asked, "Is she doing it?" The other responded, "Yes! She's singing!" There was a feeling of radiance between the two women so palpable it was an actual alleluia. I recalled one of the women mentioning she taught the second-grade religious education class. I leaned over and asked if Bella was in her class and she very proudly said, "Yes." While I knew that Bella would now have about forty overprotective father figures in her dad's firehouse, I was filled with gratitude that she would also have church ladies praying for her and cheering her on, always.

Gratitude is a word that can be overused. You can be grateful that your kid got into a good school, you can be grateful that the cop on the side of the road didn't stop you when you rolled past a stop sign, you can be grateful to find a parking spot near the door at the grocery store. And you can certainly be grateful for being unexpectedly dubbed New Yorker of the Year. I don't want to belittle these small gratitudes, but there's another kind of gratitude that gets developed when God's grace helps us through the truly challenging experiences in life. Death, sickness, despair, these are the times when gratitude anchors us. These are the times I experience gratitude at a depth I've never encountered, and I'm challenged anew to lean into it in so many contexts.

12

REALLY, GOD?
REALLY?

Love

Sport is the perfect way to get a message through to me. *Hoosiers. Bull Durham. The Bad News Bears.* Wait, *especially The Bad News Bears.* Seeing potential and achieving it, combined with slapstick and bathroom humor? Sign me up! Turns out, a simple sports analogy was the key to unlocking for me a profound understanding of what love looks like when it's practiced as a personal anchor value and when it's lived out in community.

Two leaders who have helped me put my anchor values into action while working through change and evolution in our church are Trisha Taylor and Jim Harrington. Jim used a sports analogy (my love language) to explain this process of spiritual growth. Imagine it's the beginning of the season and the coach is talking to his team. The message is this: We have the potential to be state champions—talent, opportunity, and the emotional drive to get there. But right now, we're out of shape, we're out of practice, and we aren't working together as a team. We're going to spend every minute between now and the end of the season to get from where we are to realizing our full potential as champions. But we aren't going to get there just by praying and envisioning the future. We have to put in the hard work.

Hearing this analogy, my thoughts immediately went to the Hunger Program. When we started it, we expected to serve twenty-five or thirty people, max. In the beginning, we'd sometimes wonder, Will anyone even show up today? We *did* get to twenty-five guests, and then fifty, and then a hundred, and it just kept growing. The incrementality was the killer. We were focused on taking the next right action, the tactical decisions that would get us from one week to the next. When the program got into the hundreds, we quickly realized we had a wobbly house built on a foundation never intended to hold such a big structure. It wasn't sustainable, but we had no idea how to get from where we were to where we needed to be. I kept trying to hire people, hoping to find that magic person. No amount of Christines, no one magic hire, could fix the foundation while the house continued to grow. I learned that from Jim and Trisha, and also that the same people who have the problem usually have the solution.

Even so, I did get a little magic in the person of Jacob Stewart, who worked with the Hunger Program for a time. When it was no longer bringing *me* joy like it used to, I could see it in Jacob and in the volunteers. When Jacob left, we had a heart-to-heart talk, acknowledging the facts: there was a gap between what we knew was possible in the joyful experience of sharing food and the current reality that none of us even wanted to be around the program.

I had learned an exercise called the Five Whys. I tried to use it to uncover the core truth of what we were dealing with, starting with the statement of the problem.

"I don't want to be around the Hunger Program."

Why?

"It feels like there isn't any teamwork; everyone is pulling in different directions."

Why?

"Because we're not on the same page with each other."

Why?

"Because we haven't exactly communicated our direction."

Why?

"We don't all speak the same language."

There were more whys, but you get the point. We needed to arrive at the fundamental kernel, the under-lying truth of the situation. We decided to try the Five

Whys on different aspects of the program. As we went through the stages, the finger of blame inched closer and closer toward me and my leadership. I was the problem and I needed to figure out how to fix it.

The core fix would be to establish a series of policies, procedures, and rules, communicate them to everyone and, most importantly, enforce them and reorient people to the new rules. That is a curiously spiritual process in itself. We actually had a lot of "rules," but rules that aren't enforced consistently are just suggestions. Enforcing rules isn't fun; at least I find it quite difficult. But ignoring or reshaping them at every ask is a formula for chaos. It's not loving and it definitely doesn't spark joy. Love, I was learning, sets boundaries that make us feel safe and secure; good, sensible boundaries are communicated clearly and simply.

Starting from scratch, we looked at the kind of manager we needed. We hired our current manager, Joan, because she had the mental rubrics to help us evaluate the rules. Were they fair? Were they enforceable? Were they contributing to the joy of the program? Were they structured in a way that would avoid temptation to backslide into our old ways?

As a result, for example, we created a digital ordering system for pantry orders. It helped the guests immensely, because the app listed the food in several languages and it showed pictures. It was helpful for the packers, who were now given a list rather than bagging items in front of the guest. There was no indecision when guests asked for additional items that were not allowed. The service became more equitable, and the overall anxiety decreased. Our goal was to make the program peaceful and serene. Someone once suggested that perhaps *all* hunger programs are frenetic and chaotic by nature. *No*, I said, we are not going to accept that as success. We have the team and we have the discipline to have a peaceful, serene program. True love—that mix of honesty and other values—required that I make the effort and change to do better.

Jim and Trisha taught me that living deeply from my values looks a lot like love. And that love is a verb, an expression of gratitude that inspires us to live in community and encourages us to be present and share ourselves generously. They also taught me that love is a combination of accepting *what is* at any given moment, seeing the potential for *what could be*, and then putting in the work to get there. Yes, love is at the heart of Christianity, but in a sense—and maybe this is a fastball— it's also at the heart of these anchor values: gratitude, authenticity, going big, perseverance. Love compels us to tell the truth and to do what is true—and has all kinds of practical implications.

■ ■ ■

I've learned the hard way that love involves being willing to admit your own failings and sincerely apologize. I once posted something on Facebook that, though I didn't realize it at the time, was inadvertently racist. My Facebook friend Stephen saw it and could have easily called me out in public, but instead he sent me a private message. All of a sudden, I saw it—my own racism. I was ashamed and mortified. I didn't know what to do. What I wanted to do was a combination of explain it away and delete the post altogether, acting like it never happened. Instead, I told myself that I needed to sit with it, feel it, and admit to myself that I was, indeed, racist.

A year or so later, I preached a sermon about it. It fit the Scripture reading, but it was also a means of trying to make amends. To Stephen, yes, though he was very kind and gracious from the start. I also did it because I felt like I needed to talk about white privilege and cluelessness, and that even those of us who thought we were trying our best were infected by and perpetuating the sin of racism. Love helped me make amends.

Love can also compel us to do things we wouldn't otherwise do. I've heard some people speak of foot washing as a sacramental act of love. The pope does it every Easter season, washing the feet of people as a sign of his love and his servant status to humanity. But to me, the whole idea of foot washing has always seemed bizarre and particularly *not* reformed.

To be clear: we do not touch people in our church, especially their feet. But one day, Bobby (one of my least favorite beloved children of God—remember the guy from the gratitude chapter?) came for dinner. Only he didn't eat, he just camped out on the front lawn. It was a beautiful summer day and he took his socks off, perhaps to feel the grass under his feet, or maybe just air them out. As I stood on the stoop greeting guests for dinner, the smell wafted in my direction. I called out to Bobby, asking him to put his socks on, but he said his feet hurt and couldn't he just stay outside and let them breathe a little. His feet were red and swollen, and as I looked at him this extraterrestrial urge came over me to go get a towel and wash his feet. Luckily for me, he didn't take me up on it, and I still wonder what compelled me to offer. It could only have been love.

I don't know if the sports metaphor holds, but I think of us as the church version of *The Bad News Bears*. We're a little rough around the edges, we make lots of mistakes, we're messy. But of all the things that make Greenpoint Reformed Church the place I love today, including honesty and hard work and the asking of essential Why questions, I'll say it again: it's the love of the matriarchs that is supreme. They have taught me *about* love and they have taught me *to* love. To love the church, serve the congregation. They've even shown me how to love myself. On the G train line, there's a little church that demonstrates love, not just the appreciation of love, but the definition of love as hard work. Love that addresses systemic issues that are hurtful to people. Love that addresses programs that help people flourish. Love that demands we try harder, do more, for the sake of the gospel.

13

NOBODY'S HOMELESS

Community

One day, I was hanging out near the sign-in table for the Hunger Program when I overheard someone ask a gentleman if he was homeless. "No!" he answered very confidently. I knew he lived in the park and was surprised by his answer, so I asked him where he lived. He replied, "I have a home. It's on the bench in the park," and then he gestured down the block to the playground across the street from the bodega. This interaction helped me realize that feelings of "home" do not require a physical roof and walls, but rather a sense of place and community. It's about belonging.

As humans, we form communities as a natural course. Early humans could have continued living as vagabond scavengers, but they eventually learned languages to communicate with each other and formed into small congregations, working together. As society developed, we formed into villages, kingdoms, countries, and even empires. People learned that they could accomplish more as a group than they could individually.

Life in the 21st century often pulls us further away from a sense of community. Even before the pandemic, we didn't need to gather at the local coffee shop to get the news; it was on our phones. And now more than ever, we don't have to go to the store to get food, we can have it delivered to our front door. But even with this technologically driven isolation that's only been intensified by COVID-19, we still crave human interaction. We are social animals, and being part of a society involves forming communities and experiencing a sense of belonging.

I learned at an early age that I wasn't meant to be alone. I have lots of weaknesses and knew that if I wanted to be stronger, it would take a whole community to help me learn and grow. This is, perhaps, the greatest gift of the church. It provides us with fellow travelers, people we otherwise might not know, and common ground we might not otherwise recognize. In our church, one of the things we all seem to have in common is a sense of anxiety. We're all anxious about something. But we've seen that the key is to match ourselves up with others who don't share our same anxieties, and we're able to do far more together than we ever could as individuals.

Even before pandemic-induced social distancing, some of our congregants and volunteers, like many people, had some anxiety about interacting with homeless folks. It presented a unique set of problems that required us to think differently about it than we might have otherwise. For instance, as the food pantry developed, we realized that some of our guests had kitchens and others did not. To help meet these different needs, volunteers began dividing our foodstuffs into what they called "kitchen bags" and "nonkitchen bags." The kitchen bags would contain items that needed to be refrigerated or cooked on a stove, and the nonkitchen bags would have ready-to-eat meals and food that didn't require refrigeration—things like packs of tuna and crackers, peanut butter, cereal.

Volunteers would ask guests which kind of bag they preferred. Quickly enough, volunteers developed a shorthand and began referring to the nonkitchen bags as "homeless bags." Without realizing it, they would ask guests if they had a kitchen or were homeless. With the language difficulties between English and Polish, this just seemed an easier way to get to the answer of which bag to hand them. Soon enough, though, I learned an important lesson. Nobody's homeless. There is such stigma attached to homelessness that few identify as homeless, as my conversation with the park bench resident taught me. We needed to ensure our language was an essential part of treating all our guests with respect and dignity. So that everyone, regardless of where they lay their head at night, felt a sense of belonging. As a pastor, I'm called to extend that belonging; and like the practice of love, bravery, and authenticity, belonging is something I've begun to see as another important life-giving anchor.

One day, I had just finished a very sad committal service for an FDNY colleague's son in Greenwood Cemetery. Whenever I'm near there, I think of my adopted grandma-friend-mentor-co-conspirator in fun, Carol Hageman, whom I missed sorely, so I decided to pay her a visit. I was in my FDNY chaplain's uniform and I figured I could impress her a bit. I was sure she would say my shoes were too masculine but that my freshly dry-cleaned jacket was looking good.

Carol is buried in the Old First Reformed Church section of the cemetery along with a bunch of folks who died in the 1600s and have Dutch lettering on their headstones. Carol always loved knowing she was going to be buried in Greenwood. Her husband had preached and consulted with Old First back in the 1980s, and the church didn't pay him in cash, but with a plot in the cemetery.

I too aspire to be buried here one day. It might sound odd to want to "belong" in a particular cemetery, but the neighborhood is pretty spacious and I know a few of the neighbors already. There's Carol, of course. And down the row a bit there's Dorothy Fletcher, a warm and kind woman who always brought a smile to my face at church meetings. In this restful neighborhood I am, perhaps, known for who I am: an out lesbian pastor. For that reason, while on paper I am a pastor of the United Church of Christ, there will always be a part of me that resonates with the saying *I'm RCA born and RCA bred, and when I die I'll be RCA dead.*

■ ■ ■

Our community at the church and pantry has seen many people who struggle with addiction and who live in different places, one day a park bench, the next a shelter. I've learned on many occasions that to use labels around issues of housing or homelessness can often take away a person's sense of belonging and their dignity.

One person who became part of our Greenpoint community was sweet, cantankerous, idiosyncratic Danny. He was an OG—an Original Greenpointer. And if there ever was an archetypal Greenpointer, it would be Danny. At an early age he had been diagnosed with learning disabilities. I'm not sure he ever got the care and attention he needed from the schools, or if he was actually diagnosed, but as his friend it would not have surprised me to learn that Danny was on the Autism spectrum. Although he was bright, and it looked like he should have been able to hold down a job, the truth was he could not. He would get a job, and then after a few days or weeks, something would happen and inevitably he would quit or be fired.

Danny came to the church building for AA meetings and was very proud of his sobriety. He worked hard at it and he meant well. He was always trying. And by that, I mean he was trying to do well, but he could also be a little trying to be around. Danny's status as an OG came with a rent-controlled apartment in the neighborhood, passed down through his family, so he was always out and about. A born helper, when the pantry started Danny was eagerly involved.

By Thanksgiving 2008, we were serving well over two hundred guests per week and still without the solid infrastructure we desperately needed. I had asked my parents for shelves for the food pantry for Christmas and picked out some industrial ones from Sears. I was *so excited* when the shelves arrived, I tore open the boxes, took the pieces out, and started to put them together. But *holy shit* the instructions were impossible! You might have picked up on the fact that intense focus is not one of my core competencies, and as a result, I suck at putting things together as per the instructions.

Even as a kid, while my brother would put together a LEGO set with a thousand steps in it, I would ignore the instructions and just make something else. My ADHD made many things more difficult. I thought those shelves would *never* get built and decided it was fruitless for me to try. Then, one morning, Danny came around asking if there was anything he could do to help at the church, so I showed him the shelves and he went to town. He put those things together so carefully, so meticulously, it took him two days to build all six industrial shelves, but I saw he had a real gift.

Two days before our son, John, was born, I went to lock up the church at night and discovered a box on the front steps. As I've mentioned, people often left food for the pantry, so it wasn't uncommon. But this box moved. I freaked out until I heard the mewling. It was a litter of kittens. I was in the middle of a call to go off to the hospital and Danny said to me, "Don't worry, I'll take care of the kittens." A problem solver, he then offered them to the people at the pantry. He often found a way to bring his gifts and offer help at just the right time.

As years passed, Danny became a rock in the program. However, by 2013 he had lost his apartment and become dependent on the shelter system. His preferred shelter was in Manhattan, five miles away from the church. God bless Danny, he continued to come to AA, to worship, and to the pantry, walking five miles back and forth every time. Unsurprisingly, Danny grew frustrated with the rules of the shelter system—or they got frustrated with him—and he lost his bed there, eventually resorting to a combination of couch surfing and sleeping on the subway or in the local parks. Through all of this, he continued to be a fixture in the Hunger Program and in our AA ministry.

One night, after hunkering down and watching *The Good Wife* (next to my own good wife), I went downstairs to make sure the church was locked up. For the first time in ten years, I heard someone in the church. A dude snoring. I quietly freaked out and ran upstairs to call—who *should* I call? I called the cops, then I got a piece of wood that roughly approximated a baseball bat and started planning how to beat whomever it was to a pulp, assuming he would ultimately attack my family. New York's Finest finally showed up and, after a quick investigation, discovered the snoring dude to be—Danny. It was his birthday, and he'd come to church for worship that morning. We had celebrated with brownies and then he hung around for the seven p.m. meeting. He was so tired he had fallen asleep on the pew during the meeting and only woke up when the cops turned on the light.

He was scared. I was scared. The cops looked to me, and I decided that I would prefer to leave Danny on the pew rather than toss him out of the sanctuary. I told him it was getting cold out and that it was about time we made a plan for the winter. He agreed and we planned to go to the intake shelter the next day. I closed up the church and went back upstairs. I logged into my pastor's prayer circle, a Facebook group, and posted the story of discovering Danny. I ended my prayers with this:

> Today is Danny's birthday. Please pray for him. That he might humble himself to go back and ask for his spot at the shelter. And that he might get the help he needs. He can't really make it on his own. And please offer a prayer of thanksgiving that I don't have a gun and that I didn't beat him to a pulp with my quasi-baseball bat.

Prayers flowed in online from my pastor friends. That night, I had a deep sense that Danny (and I) were enveloped in prayers, the love of Greenpoint, the love of my pastor friends, and God's love. I also had a deep sense that we belonged to each other.

The next morning, when I went downstairs to check on Danny, he was lying peacefully on a church pew. And when I say "peacefully," I mean Danny was enjoying the Lord's eternal peace. Sometime during that night Danny had died. I freaked out, said a quick prayer, and went upstairs to beg my wife for help. Between the church and FDNY, I conduct and attend many funerals and visit those who are dying, but she is the true responsible pastor in the family when it comes to things like death. After all of the logistics had been taken care of, I had a moment to reflect on Danny's last night: the songs and brownies we shared on his birthday, how he'd spent the day under the shelter of the sanctuary and in a canopy of prayer. On his last day, he was home, he was with us. I wept for our loss, and I felt joy that he had, at last, found a permanent place to belong.

Whenever I think about homelessness and the labels we attach to people, I think about Danny and his many homes and communities, the places where he experienced belonging: the food pantry, the AA program, and, as an OG, the neighborhood. One final memory of Danny stays with me: he loved taking inventory of the canned goods in the food pantry, but he was so precise that if he ended up one can off, he would do a recount and couldn't be finished until he had the *exact* number of cans. He kept count on the back of the door of the pantry room, which he had painted with chalkboard paint. If you come to Greenpoint you can still see Danny's last inventory count. Having it there fulfills my need to keep a little part of him alive and affirm that this was a place where he belonged.

14

EVERYTHING IS FIXABLE

Hope

As a pastor and chaplain and someone who believes that love is the practical value that allows us to accept the work we're given, to look at ourselves honestly, to live generously, and to better ourselves and our communities, I also understand that love is inextricably tied to hope. We love and therefore have hope for our community—our neighbors, our families, and our friends—to experience God's *eternal* love, in the afterlife and in our daily lives. Without hope, life is meaningless. Hope sees a future. It believes that things can change, that we are not doomed to our present reality. Hope is what we most search for, yearn for, rely upon.

Anyone who has raised a child knows there are times when hope does not spring eternal, and that it sometimes comes in bite-sized chunks. Maybe it starts with "God, please let me have a baby," followed by "God, please let this baby be healthy." And then, once the baby is born, your hope horizon is both wide and narrow, depending on the day. It might be "Please let my baby grow to be a happy, healthy contributor to society," or simply "Please help me find her lost blankie so she'll stop screaming."

When your baby turns two or three, you will pray fervently to get him or her potty trained. (Don't act surprised; you knew this wouldn't be a good pastor story without a little shit.) One Sunday we baptized a two-year-old named Nora. The following day, she announced to her mom, Amanda, "Mama, I baptized. I go to Sunday school. I big girl. I no diapers." And then potty trained herself. Anyone who has experienced the pain of potty training a toddler will immediately recognize in this miraculous story how the Holy Spirit can conquer anything, and will commence fervently hoping and praying for that same inspiration for their own toddler.

Not just potty training: I have an unshakable belief that the Holy Spirit can truly fix anything. Yes, people die. Yes, we experience pain. Job losses. Divorce. Yes, our lives can be changed in an instant. You can be cut from your denomination because of your same-gender relationship. Or taken out of church leadership for officiating at your gay daughter's wedding. We some-times feel caught, desperate, squeezed. Hope—and love and bravery and authenticity—are practices we live into, they are value-muscles that you build, little by little. You practice. And you keep practicing.

If I've learned anything about anchor values, and especially hope, it's that they are best understood and lived out in the context of our day-to-day, ordinary steps of faith, not in our grasp of complex theological concepts.

By the time I entered my senior year of seminary, I was starting to feel uncomfortable with my personal inability to sign off on what seemed to be a necessary belief in what theologians call "substitutionary atone-ment." One night, in our New Testament class, I thought it would be prudent to raise my hand and bluntly ask my deep, dark question: "If God is sovereign over all, why exactly did Jesus have to die for my sins?" I might as well have farted loudly at a high society holiday party. My fellow students didn't know whether to gape at me in horror or look away; most settled on the judgmental look of the True Christian.

One seminarian literally gasped out loud, saying, "You can't ask that question. You're the daughter of the president of the seminary!"

In my insecurity, I stammered "But, you know . . . people in our churches are going to ask us. And I don't know what to say. Because I don't know why he had to die."

Thankfully, Professor Virginia Wiles was thrilled at such theological upheaval. In spite of the responses of my classmates, she delighted in having the chance to explain her personal understanding of the atonement: it was her contention that Jesus's death was actually one of the easier parts to understand about the Holy Week story. Jesus, she explained, experienced the full range of awful things that life brings to human beings. He was sold out by his friend, he was denied three times by another friend, he was mocked and ridiculed, he was put on trial for trumped-up charges. Then, he watched as a hardened criminal was released from prison while he, the innocent one, was condemned to die. And he was humiliated *in front of his mother*.

Professor Wiles went on to explain that if we believe that God became human in the form of Jesus of Nazareth, then we can believe that God experienced all the horrible, painful, difficult things we experience. When we are in the middle of our worst times, we can call upon a God who knows our pain. When God, in Christ, goes into the grave, we are assured that God suffers with us when we face our own graves, or when we feel dead inside, or when we wish we were dead. We are assured, we have faith, that God goes with us into our deepest and most painful experiences, and that nothing separates us from the love or the presence of God.

This explanation resonated deeply with me, then and now. Jesus's resurrection gives us hope that nothing is impossible. Nothing is unfixable. That hope and joy and love win out over fear and anger and desperation. Living by this value means that we can turn from focusing on the worst-case scenario and embrace God's call for us to live bigger. To love bolder. To forgive more often.

Taking it a step further, I began to think that maybe hope is also about knowing ourselves and living into that knowledge. In his book *New Seeds of Contemplation*, Thomas Merton observed that *a tree gives glory to God by being a tree*. I often recite this phrase like a mantra in my head as a reminder that my only job is to be my most authentic self. I've discovered that the more I embrace the person God made me, the more I'm able to love God. And, really, that's the only thing I can offer to God and to the world.

A few years ago, I had the honor of meeting a fancy bishop. One of my Catholic clergy friends graciously escorted me over to the Right Reverend and introduced me. The bishop shook my hand, squished up his already wrinkled face, turned his head slightly to the right and looked over my shoulder so as not to make eye contact.

He looked as though he had bitten into a juicy orange slice only to discover it was actually a lemon. Perhaps this is the way he greeted all his visitors. Or maybe I gave him momentary indigestion. Protestants and Catholics don't mix very well in New York City, and I can only imagine that a queer female Protestant minister might not have sparked joy inside that particular bishop. It happens.

I found it more funny than painful, but my joyful, fun-loving Catholic friend appeared heartbroken. "I'm sorry he's a turd, Ann," he said.

I replied, "Thomas Merton says a tree gives glory to God by being a tree. So maybe that's all the bishop's got and he's giving God glory by being a turd?"

"Well, then. He's offering God the turdliest of turds," he said.

There was something particularly heartwarming about a stately, dignified Monsignor proclaiming a bishop to be the "turdliest." It wasn't mean spirited, more factually descriptive. And it placed the three of us—me, the bishop, and the Monsignor—in the same relationship to God. It also fit with my *Stand up for total depravity* viewpoint quite nicely.

There's a story in the gospels that helps me understand the "treeness of the tree" and speaks to truth and to faith. In John's Gospel, a blind man was healed by Jesus. Some Pharisees asked the man (several times) how he received his sight and who he perceived the healer to be. The man answered, saying, essentially, I cannot tell you who this man Jesus is. I can only tell you that I once was blind and now I see. This whole book is an attempt to talk about the healing power of Jesus. But like the blind man, I don't know how it all works. Nor do I know what it means that Jesus-died-for-all. All I know is that I used to be broken and now I am more whole.

The tension among Christians over what they perceive as the "Truth" about why Jesus died is something I just don't get. I did not grow up in an evangelical milieu, nor did I attend a Christian college. To be honest, it seems as if "Truth" is part of a coded language evangelicals use and I don't understand. Like the rapture and homeschooling—it's something evangelicals talk about that doesn't weigh particularly heavily on my mind. Being asked to cough up or claim "the Truth" as a litmus test for one's faith is a test that has eluded me. No matter what I might say, I have the sneaking suspicion that I'm going to answer incorrectly.

Maybe it's because I've learned something about values like authenticity, hope, holy shit, and Holy Spirit Goggles, and I realize it's not about passing a test. It's about practices. It's about devotion, not to a set of beliefs or dogma, but to God and to the people God puts in my path. If you asked me about my faith in Jesus, I could write a love letter that might never end. I believe in the Truth of Jesus, and yet I am not sure how to define Truth or how to evangelical-speak the correct answer on Atonement. Living with questions, allowing for mysteries we may never grasp, maybe that comes with the territory of being people called to live by faith. It certainly doesn't mean our hope is any less robust.

My work as a chaplain with the Fire Department of New York has taught me more about fundamental Truth than any other job. I've learned that the bravest thing our people do is raise their right hand and take an oath to protect the life and property of the city of New York. And when someone in our city cries out for help, dedicated EMTs, paramedics, and firefighters respond immediately. In those moments, these civil servants do not have the luxury of philosophical debates about the definition of Truth—they are on a relentless mission to search for life and save it. They show their love for God and neighbor not by their words but by their actions. Perhaps it's in these life-and-death moments when we come face-to-face with the most fundamental Truth, not a conceptual one. Everything falls away, and we are left with our own mortality reflected back in the face of a fellow human being.

Living out this kind of truth is not without a cost—running in when others run out means experiencing trauma, again and again. It means being present when life is at its most broken and painful. It takes a toll on a person's mind and soul. Someone on the FDNY team once told me about some of his experiences and, in the process, gave me the gift of his own fundamental truth. He leaned in and said in a raspy voice, "You know, Reverend, we're all f*$#@d up around here. But we're all f*$#@d up together."

Even in—and especially in—your most painful moments, I yearn to offer wise words and want them to be words of hope: the fundamental Truth is that we are all broken, and we are broken together. The story of Jesus on the cross is the story of being broken together. The story of Easter is that same story with an additional note: everything is fixable. It's the hope that compels me to take bold risks, even if I might flop, even if I screw up.

It's the hope that even in the midst of his deepest pain, Danny could take care of kittens and build shelves for us. That he could live in community and find rest in the sanctuary of a church.

It's the hope that Christine could commandeer the food kitchen and save it, and that, in the wake of losing her, we could rebuild it into something even more beautiful.

It's the hope that a church with a three-people attendance (six, if you count the Father, Son, and Holy Spirit) and three praying matriarchs could provide food to a hungry neighborhood and raise a banner challenging that neighborhood to live better together.

It's the hope that leads me to believe that even the shit on our church stoop is holy.

It's the hope in my every prayer for the firefighters who are taking their last breaths from the toll 9/11 took on their bodies.

And it's a hope for you, and for me. Wherever we are, whatever we feel called to, that we can bring our authentic, brave selves into our neighborhoods, in service to our small towns, our cities, and believe that we can be part of making change.